My Word

My Word

Favourite Bible Passages of Famous People

Compiled and edited
by Diana Parsk

Hodder & Stoughton
LONDON SYDNEY AUCKLAND

First published in Great Britain in 2002

10 9 8 7 6 5 4 3 2 1

British Library Cataloguing in Publication Data
A record for this book is available from the British Library

ISBN 0 340 78705 8

Typeset by Avon Dataset Ltd, Bidford-on-Avon, Warks

Printed and bound in Great Britain by
Bookmarque

Hodder & Stoughton
A Division of Hodder Headline Ltd
338 Euston Road
London NW1 3BH

www.madaboutbooks.com

This book is dedicated to

R. M. J. – with all my love

My children – Stephanie, Nicholas, Rosalind, Eleanor, Annabel, Lucinda and Christianne – for their love and support, always

My parents – Peggy and Joe Houghton – for always being there for me

Special thanks to

Linda Lowes – for so willingly doing all the typing for me

Theresa O'Malley – for her encouragement and practical help

The Holy Bible

God inspired, the Holy Word
Spirit soaring like a bird
Infuses soul and heart and head
Transforms to life from parchment dead.

Cradle of Christians and of Jews
Warning of evil, proclaiming Good News.
Precursor of Islam, belief in one God
History of land where one people once trod.

A source of comfort, peace and light
Gives the spiritually blind a new hope of sight.
Guiding us all through the darkest night
To God's Holy City, shining and bright.

R. M. Jordan

Contents

Foreword

The Bible is the supreme source document of Christianity but it is not the private property of Christians. It has a power and a pertinence for people of every kind and in every age. It speaks about God but it also speaks from God and concerns itself with the struggles, tragedies, aspirations and destiny of humanity itself. This has given it a contemporary relevance across the centuries and enabled it to be a light on the journey of life for all humankind.

It is that conviction which inspired Diana Parsk's imaginative project for her pupils at St Bede's Ecumenical School. What began as a local endeavour has touched a chord that resonates with the experience of many people across a wide spectrum of society, whose lives have been influenced by the Bible.

Her book is a poignant testimony to that fact. It is an admirable achievement and one which, I feel, will bring encouragement, inspiration and comfort to many people.

Above all, perhaps, it is a salutary reminder, in a rather materialistic age, that 'One does not live by bread alone, but by every word that comes from the mouth of God'.

Roy Williamson
Bishop of Bradford (1984–91)
Bishop of Southwark (1991–98)

Preface

As a mother of seven children and a teacher of Religious Education at St Bede's Ecumenical School in Redhill, Surrey, I have the responsibility and challenge of bringing alive the words of the Holy Bible and explaining their relevance to life today. This is not always readily accepted by pupils who are being raised in an exciting technological world where science is now able to explain many of the mysteries of creation itself. However, there is still a spiritual dimension to life, the foundation of which is faith. This faith is reflected in the thoughts and activities of individuals and it is they who witness to the relevance and power of the words of the Holy Bible.

In reflecting on how I could demonstrate that the Bible is still the living word and relevant to our daily life, I had the idea of writing to personalities in the public eye and asking them to tell me what their favourite Bible passage is and what it means to them. My list was, of course, my own personal selection. I included leading politicians, actors, musicians, radio and television personalities, sports winners, popular authors and religious leaders at both national and local level. I am very grateful to the many who replied, usually in their own handwriting, and for their words of encouragement. Some selected more than one passage, others gave me their current favourite and explained that their choice varies from time to time according to circumstances. A few did not give a reason for their choice but I have included their selection because they are people of particular interest or prominence. The majority, however, despite leading very busy lives, made the time to explain to me and my pupils how the words of the Bible are a source of inspiration, guidance and comfort to them.

The replies have had a huge impact on my pupils, and so I thought that their choices and comments would be of a wider interest. Also through publication as a book, they would encourage the reading of the Bible and in addition raise money for charity, as I am very pleased to say that royalties from the sale of this book will go to Christian Aid.

In addition to thanking everyone who took the time and trouble to reply to me, I should like to acknowledge the help and encouragement I received in compiling this book from my family, friends and colleagues.

I hope that you, dear reader, will also find inspiration in this book and will be encouraged to reflect on your own favourite Bible passages and what they mean to you.

Diana Parsk

Acknowledgments

Extracts from the Authorised Version of the Bible (AV, the King James Bible), the rights in which are vested in the Crown, are reproduced by permission of the Crown's Patentee, Cambridge University Press.

Scriptures quoted from the Good News Bible (GNB) published by the Bible Societies/HarperCollins Publishers Ltd., UK © American Bible Society, 1966, 1971, 1976, 1992.

Extracts taken from the Jerusalem Bible (JB), published and copyright 1966, 1967 and 1968 by Darton, Longman & Todd Ltd. and Doubleday & Co. Inc. and used by permission of the publishers.

New English Bible (NEB) © Oxford University Press and Cambridge University Press, 1961, 1970.

Scripture quotations marked (NIV) are taken from the Holy Bible New International Version ® NIV ®. Copyright © 1973, 1978, 1984 by International Bible Society. Used by permission. All rights preserved.

Scripture quotations from the New Revised Standard Version (NRSV), copyright © 1989 by the Division of Christian Education of the National Council of the Churches of Christ in the USA. Used by permission. All rights preserved.

Revised English Bible (REB) © Oxford University Press and Cambridge University Press, 1989.

THE OLD TESTAMENT

Genesis 1:1–5, 20, 25, 29–31

In the beginning God created the heaven and the earth.

And the earth was without form, and void; and the darkness was upon the face of the deep. And the Spirit of God moved upon the face of the waters.

And God said, Let there be light: and there was light.

And God saw the light, that it was good: and God divided the light from the darkness.

And God called the light Day, and the darkness he called Night. And the evening and the morning were the first day . . .

And God said, Let the waters bring forth abundantly the moving creature that hath life, and fowl that may fly above the earth in the open firmament of heaven . . .

And God made the beast of the earth after his kind, and cattle after their kind, and every thing that creepeth upon the earth after his kind: and God saw that it was good . . .

And God said, Behold, I have given you every herb bearing seed, which is upon the face of all the earth, and every tree, in the which is the fruit of a tree yielding seed; to you it shall be for meat.

And to every beast of the earth, and to every fowl of the air, and to every thing that creepeth upon the earth, wherein there is life, I have given every green herb for meat; and it was so.

And God saw every thing that he had made, and, behold, it was very good. And the evening and the morning were the sixth day. (AV)

Nickolas Grace

Actor and Director

This passage creates an incredible picture in the reader's and listener's mind. Additionally, the words are carefully chosen, and beautiful to speak. It must, of course, be the King James version. I love reading aloud from the Bible in churches and cathedrals. The power of the spoken word is uplifting.

Lucinda Green

Writer and Rider

Verse 1 encompasses in one short sentence the core of my belief: that there is an infinite power, that the world and those of us in it are *not* a creation of physics.

Penelope Keith

Actress

I chose verses 29 to 31 because I am a gardener.

The Revd Professor Mary Seller

Professor of Developmental Genetics, The Guy's, King's and St Thomas Hospitals' School of Medicine, London, and Assistant Priest at St John the Evangelist, Hurst Green, Surrey

I have chosen verses 20 and 25 because the natural world that God has created is so wonderful. The enormous variety of animal life that exists exceeds anything that we could ever devise ourselves, or even imagine. Television programmes open our eyes to some of this diversity. In the depths of the oceans are astonishing fishes with enormous gaping jaws, and curious tentacled worms, while in the waters above there are graceful jellyfish, delicate seahorses, and gigantic whales feeding on the myriad of tiny planktonic creatures, as well as all the teeming fish. On land and in the air, sloths and armadillos, monkeys and elephants, humming-birds and kingfishers, eagles and penguins, bats and butterflies, frogs and snakes, millipedes and ladybirds all occupy their own particular habitats. All so different, all so beautiful.

But recent studies in molecular genetics reveal something equally wonderful and astonishing. At the level of the DNA, there is enormous conservation of both gene sequence and gene function between species. Genes are the chemical instructions for making the structure of our bodies and for their function. The processes of development from a fertilised egg to an adult are controlled by genes, and many of these genes are exactly the same in humans and in mice and in flies and in worms, and probably in all animals if all animals were examined. A specific mouse gene can be engineered into the larva of a fly, and it directs the correct development of the fly, and vice versa. Thus there seems to be a basic, genetic body-building kit that has been retained for millions and millions of years and used over and over again to make the bodies of all the different animals, birds, fish, insects and creeping things. However, what is not yet known is how this basic body plan is developed and extended to produce the multitude of different forms of animal life we see. That is bound to be yet another marvel of God's creation.

The Rt. Hon. Lord Norman Tebbit, CH

Former Tory Party Chairman and Trade and Industry Secretary

The first chapter of Genesis is the most remarkable and significant part of the Bible. Written long before science had begun to unravel the history of creation, it sets out the story of creation not merely in the most remarkable prose (in the King James version) but in the correct chronological order as subsequently confirmed by science.

Penny Vincenzi

Author

I have chosen this passage because it paints so glorious and vivid a picture, gives such a sense of power and majesty and beauty that it is able to instil a sense of awe into *us*, believers or not.

~

Genesis 3:1–6, 9–12, 22–23

Now the serpent was more subtil than any beast of the field which the Lord God had made. And he said unto the woman, Yea, hath God said, Ye shall not eat of every tree of the garden?

And the woman said unto the serpent, We may eat of the fruit of the trees of the garden:

But of the fruit of the tree which is in the midst of the garden, God hath said, Ye shall not eat of it, neither shall ye touch it, lest ye die.

And the serpent said unto the woman, Ye shall not surely die:

For God doth know that in the day ye eat thereof, then your eyes shall be opened, and ye shall be as gods, knowing good and evil.

And when the woman saw that the tree was good for food, and that it was pleasant to the eyes, and a tree to be desired to make one wise, she took of the fruit thereof, and did eat, and gave also unto her husband with her; and he did eat . . .

And the Lord God called unto Adam, and said unto him, Where art thou?

And he said, I heard thy voice in the garden, and I was afraid, because I was naked; and I hid myself.

And he said, Who told thee that thou wast naked? Hast thou eaten of the tree, whereof I commanded thee that thou shouldest not eat?

And the man said, The woman whom thou gavest to be with me, she gave me of the tree, and I did eat . . .

And the Lord God said, Behold, the man is become as one of us, to know good and evil: and now, lest he put forth his hand, and take also of the tree of life, and eat, and live for ever:

Therefore the Lord God sent him forth from the garden of Eden, to till the ground from whence he was taken. (AV)

Shirley Hughes

Author and Illustrator

The Fall is one of the strongest images of the Old Testament which, along with the story of the Flood, lodges indelibly in the memory from early childhood. The poetic language, particularly from the King James version, is unforgettable. I have just attempted to retell it for very young children, as a 'story within a story' in my picture book, *Alfie Weather*.

Genesis 18:19

For I have chosen him, so that he will direct his children and his household after him to keep the way of the Lord by doing what is right and just, so that the Lord will bring about for Abraham what he has promised him. (NIV)

James Fox

Actor

To receive such a promise from God concerning the future was a privilege for Abraham and shows the faithfulness of God, for he fulfilled it and is still fulfilling it down to today.

~

Genesis 28:16

Yahweh is in this place and I never knew it! (JB)

The Revd Ruth Scott
Priest, Writer and Broadcaster
This verse sums up my experience so profoundly. Time and again I've been surprised by God in people and situations where I did not expect God to be; even, dare I say it, at the heart of my own wounds. When I venture into new territory that verse is my guiding light, reminding me that God is not confined by my limitations of understanding.

Genesis 39:20–21

But while Joseph was there in the prison, the LORD was with him; he showed him kindness and granted him favour in the eyes of the prison warder. (NIV)

THE REVD DAVID POWE

SENIOR CHAPLAIN AT HER MAJESTY'S PRISON, BELMARSH

In Belmarsh Prison we get through thousands of Bibles as all the prisoners want to read the Scriptures and God has been so good in bringing so many to himself. I always show this passage from Genesis to the prisoners to remind them that God will be with them in Belmarsh, that is if they want him to be. We now have to provide the Bible in forty different languages, ranging from Persian to Chinese and Urdu.

Exodus 20:1–17

And God spake all these words, saying,

I am the Lord thy God, which have brought thee out of the land of Egypt, out of the house of bondage.

Thou shalt have no other gods before me.

Thou shalt not make unto thee any graven image, or any likeness of any thing that is in heaven above, or that is in the earth beneath, or that is in the water under the earth:

Thou shalt not bow down thyself to them, nor serve them: for I the Lord thy God am a jealous God, visiting the iniquity of the fathers upon the children unto the third and fourth generation of them that hate me;

And shewing mercy unto thousands of them that love me, and keep my commandments.

Thou shalt not take the name of the Lord thy God in vain; for the Lord will not hold him guiltless that taketh his name in vain.

Remember the sabbath day, to keep it holy.

Six days shalt thou labour, and do all thy work:

But the seventh day is the sabbath of the Lord thy God: in it thou shalt not do any work, thou, nor thy son, nor thy daughter, thy manservant, nor thy maidservant, nor thy cattle, nor thy stranger that is within thy gates:

For in six days the Lord made heaven and earth, the sea, and all that in them is, and rested the seventh day: wherefore the Lord blessed the sabbath day, and hallowed it.

Honour thy father and thy mother: that thy days may be long upon the land which the Lord thy God giveth thee.

Thou shalt not kill.

Thou shalt not commit adultery.

Thou shalt not steal.

Thou shalt not bear false witness against thy neighbour.

Thou shalt not covet thy neighbour's house, thou shalt not covet thy neighbour's wife, nor his manservant, nor his maidservant, nor his ox, nor his ass, nor anything that is thy neighbour's. (AV)

Jean Alexander
Actress
These are the guidelines by which I try to live my life.

This passage was also chosen by
Lord Jeffrey Archer
Writer

Leviticus 19:18

Thou shalt love thy neighbour as thyself. (AV)

Felicity Kendal
Actress
I look at the Bible from a Jewish viewpoint. If implemented, this concept would save our world from war and jealousy, greed and cruelty.

~

Joshua 1:1–9

Now after the death of Moses the servant of the Lord it came to pass, that the Lord spake unto Joshua the son of Nun, Moses' minister, saying,

Moses my servant is dead; now therefore arise, go over this Jordan, thou, and all this people, unto the land which I do give to them, even to the children of Israel.

Every place that the sole of your foot shall tread upon, that have I given unto you, as I said unto Moses.

From the wilderness and this Lebanon even unto the great river, the river Euphrates, all the land of the Hittites, and unto the great sea toward the going down of the sun, shall be your coast.

There shall not any man be able to stand before thee all the days of thy life: as I was with Moses, so I will be with thee: I will not fail thee, nor forsake thee.

Be strong and of a good courage: for unto this people shalt thou divide for an inheritance the land, which I sware unto their fathers to give them.

Only be thou strong and very courageous, that thou mayest observe to do according to all the law, which Moses my servant commanded thee: turn not from it to the right hand or to the left, that thou mayest prosper whithersoever thou goest.

This book of the law shall not depart out of thy mouth; but thou shalt meditate therein day and night, that thou mayest observe to do according to all that is written therein: for then thou shalt make thy way prosperous, and then thou shalt have good success.

Have I not commanded thee? Be strong and of a good courage; be not afraid, neither be thou dismayed: for the Lord thy God is with thee whithersoever thou goest. (AV)

Dr Stephanie Cook, BM, B.Ch., MA

Athlete and Doctor

Modern Pentathlon Olympic Gold Medallist

Verse 9 gives me courage and reminds me that my strength comes from God and that he is always with me to guide me, particularly through the darker moments in life.

David Dimbleby

Presenter

This was the lesson read at the end of every term at my first school. I still find it moving.

David Suchet

Actor

In our world today, full of materialistic values and a desire for instant gratification in all things, it is sometimes very hard both personally and professionally to swim against the tide. Verse 9 gives so much needed courage.

Joshua 10:25

Do not be afraid or dismayed; be strong and of good courage. (RSV)

and

Isaiah 30:15

In quietness and in trust shall be your strength. (RSV)

Katie Boyle (Lady Saunders)
Columnist
Not only have these words been of immense encouragement to me personally, but I have shared them with many folk (and not only practising Christians) who have told me that they have been ideas to 'hang on to' when necessary. Fear has been described as the greatest threat to health, happiness and peace in our generation, simply because fear is so widespread – and is a great deceiver and destroyer, not only of personal tranquillity (by robbing our minds of peace) but also at the international level by breaking relationships, both at the personal and collective levels. Fear goads us into impulsive, foolish and sometimes violent action; there is a 'paralysis' about fear which numbs our ability to think, to trust and to love. Courage, quietness and trust really are the means by which we can overcome it.

1 Samuel 17:32, 40, 45–47, 49–50

And David said to Saul, Let no man's heart fail because of him; thy servant will go and fight with this Philistine . . .

And he took his staff in his hand, and chose him five smooth stones out of the brook, and put them in a shepherd's bag which he had, even in a scrip; and his sling was in his hand: and he drew near to the Philistine . . .

Then said David to the Philistine, Thou comest to me with a sword, and with a spear, and with a shield: but I come to thee in the name of the LORD of hosts, the God of the armies of Israel, whom thou hast defied.

This day will the LORD deliver thee into mine hand; and I will smite thee, and take thine head from thee; and I will give the carcases of the host of the Philistines this day unto the fowls of the air, and to the wild beasts of the earth; that all the earth may know that there is a God in Israel.

And all this assembly shall know that the LORD saveth not with sword and spear: for the battle is the LORD's, and he will give you into our hands . . .

And David put his hand in his bag, and took thence a stone, and slang it, and smote the Philistine in his forehead, that the stone sunk into his forehead; and he fell upon his face to the earth.

So David prevailed over the Philistine with a sling and with a stone, and smote the Philistine, and slew him; but there was no sword in the hand of David. (AV)

Lesley Pearse

Writer

I like it because I have always believed that the little man can triumph over the big one, providing he has right on his side. One can apply the belief to almost any walk of life, any goal, it isn't really about fighting. There were people who told me I had no chance of ever getting published, let alone becoming a best-selling writer. But I persisted, and I made it.

Esther 4:16; 7:3–4; 9:24–25

Go, gather together all the Jews that are present in Shushan, and fast ye for me, and neither eat nor drink three days, night or day: I also and my maidens will fast likewise; and so will I go in unto the king, which is not according to the law: and if I perish, I perish . . .

Then Esther the queen answered and said, If I have found favour in thy sight, O king, and if it please the king, let my life be given me at my petition, and my people at my request.

For we are sold, I and my people, to be destroyed, to be slain, and to perish. But if we had been sold for bondmen and bondwomen, I had held my tongue, although the enemy could not countervail the king's damage . . .

Because Haman the son of Hammedatha, the Agagite, the enemy of all the Jews, had devised against the Jews to destroy them, and had cast Pur, that is, the lot, to consume them, and to destroy them;

But when Esther came before the king, he commanded by letters that his wicked device, which he devised against the Jews, should return upon his own head, and that he and his sons should be hanged on the gallows. (AV)

Esther Rantzen

Broadcaster and Chair of Childline

It is a very exciting story. She was a clever, liberated woman who married a king and saved her people.

Job 29:21–25

Unto me men gave ear, and waited, and kept silence at my counsel.

After my words they spake not again; and my speech dropped upon them.

And they waited for me as for the rain; and they opened their mouth wide as for the latter rain.

If I laughed on them, they believed it not; and the light of my countenance they cast not down.

I chose out their way, and sat chief, and dwelt as a king in the army, as one that comforteth the mourners. (AV)

Adrian Plass

Writer and Speaker

It is a model for all Christian speakers, particularly the suggestion that people should see the smile of God in the words and faces of those who minister to them.

~

Psalm 1:1

Happy are those who reject the advice of evil men,
who do not follow the example of sinners
or join those who have no use for God. (GNB)

Sir James Galway, KBVO, OBE

Musician

Good advice for living a disciplined life – much needed in this world we are living in.

Psalm 8

O Lord our Lord, how excellent is thy name in all the earth! who hast set thy glory above the heavens.

Out of the mouth of babes and sucklings hast thou ordained strength because of thine enemies, that thou mightest still the enemy and the avenger.

When I consider thy heavens, the work of thy fingers, the moon and the stars, which thou hast ordained;

What is man, that thou art mindful of him? and the son of man, that thou visitest him?

For thou hast made him a little lower than the angels, and hast crowned him with glory and honour.

Thou madest him to have dominion over the works of thy hands; thou hast put all things under his feet.

All sheep and oxen, yea and the beasts of the field;

The fowl of the air, and the fish of the sea, and whatsoever passeth through the paths of the seas.

O Lord our Lord, how excellent is thy name in all the earth! (AV)

Kriss Akabusi, MBE, MA

Motivational Speaker

It is incredible to think that the infinite God is interested in finite man. So often in everyday life the high and mighty look down on the poor and disenfranchised – not so the omnipotent God.

~

Psalm 16:11

Thou wilt shew me the path of life: in thy presence is fulness of joy; at thy right hand there are pleasures for evermore. (AV)

Prebendary Dr Chad Varah, CH, CBE, MA (Oxon), DSC

Rector of St Stephen Walbrook, City of London, and Founder of the Samaritans

It is positive, not condemnatory or prudish or exalting misery.

Psalm 23

The LORD is my shepherd; I shall not want.

He maketh me to lie down in green pastures: he leadeth me beside the still waters.

He restoreth my soul: he leadeth me in the paths of righteousness for his name's sake.

Yea, though I walk through the valley of the shadow of death, I will fear no evil: for thou art with me; thy rod and thy staff they comfort me.

Thou preparest a table before me in the presence of mine enemies: thou anointest my head with oil; my cup runneth over.

Surely goodness and mercy shall follow me all the days of my life: and I will dwell in the house of the LORD for ever. (AV)

THE RT. HON. DAVID DAVIS, MP
It is one of the most inspirational pieces of writing I have ever seen.

RANULF FIENNES
BRITISH TRAVEL WRITER, LECTURER AND EXPLORER
Great words and comforting.

TRISHA GODDARD
TV PRESENTER
This passage was such a great comfort to me when I was very ill in hospital.

Sarah Greene

Presenter

We sang the hymn version of this psalm practically every day at primary school, so I enjoy the associations and the memories. As a psalm or even a poem, it contains some of the most comforting lines ever written – appropriate whatever your beliefs.

The Revd Paul Hulme

Methodist Minister at New River Circuit, North London, and Broadcaster

Formerly Superintendent Minister at Wesley's Chapel, London, 1988–96

I have chosen verse 4 because God is there for us, not only in the good times, but in the experiences of darkness as well. Perhaps, not least, in the darkness. For, in Jesus, he is a God who knows what it feels like to be human. His agonising cry in the darkness of Calvary was 'My God, my God, why have you forsaken me?' And because he has been there for us, he will help us to endure it. And bring us through.

Mike Perkins

Deputy Head, St Bede's School, Redhill, Surrey

The psalm provides an important sense of security and certainty for the future in what is a very insecure and uncertain world. It is very reassuring and expresses fundamental confidence in the Lord.

Peter Polycarpou

Actor

When things seem at their bleakest or life seems to be telling you there is nothing to look forward to, it is comforting to know that we can trust in something greater than the total of all our worries. Trust is the way children offer themselves to our care. We are all children of God's love.

Anna Quayle

Actress and Writer

This beautiful psalm encapsulates all that I need to carry with me through the day – hope, human dignity and safety in the certain knowledge of redemption.

Dame Cicely Saunders

Retired Medical Doctor, Former Nurse and Social Worker and Founder of the Hospice Movement

I read the psalms daily, remembering that Jesus said them and prayed with them throughout his life and in his death. They express all our hopes and fears and confidence and suit every occasion. Psalm 23 is so often used with hospice patients and families.

Psalm 27:1

The Lord is my light and my salvation;
whom shall I fear?
The Lord is the stronghold of my life;
of whom shall I be afraid? (NRSV)

Don McLean
Comedian and Radio Presenter
Being a Christian means never having to be afraid. I am confident that God is looking after me. In life there are people you encounter who attempt to make you look small but I shall never shrink because God is by my side.

~

Psalm 31:8

You have set my feet in a broad place. (NRSV)

and

John 10:10

I came that they may have life, and have it abundantly. (NRSV)

and

Romans 8:38–39

For I am convinced that neither death, nor life, nor angels, nor rulers, nor things present, nor things to come, nor powers, nor height, nor depth, nor anything else in all creation, will be able to separate us from the love of God in Christ Jesus our Lord. (NRSV)

The Rt. Revd Michael Langrish
The Bishop of Exeter
Each of these verses speak of what is at the heart of my faith. This is God as he has revealed himself through Jesus. He has shown himself to be constantly at work, helping people to be more truly themselves, more truly human, setting them free from the hurts, the pains, the failures and all those other things which cramp and limit human life.

Psalm 34:8

O taste and see that the LORD is good: blessed is the man that trusteth in him. (AV)

THE RT. REVD JONATHAN BAILEY
THE BISHOP OF DERBY
It is my experience; and my vocation, long before my ordination and since, has been to urge and encourage others to discover this for themselves so they will be changed. In turn they will then work to change the world.

Psalm 46:10

Be still, and know that I am God. (AV)

Dora Bryan

Actress

It sums me up, to be still, is not easy for me. But essential and so rewarding.

James Grout

Actor

It says it all. It defines prayer. It has a wonderful economy. It has a serenity that covers and counteracts any tense situation. It helps.

The Rt. Revd Tim Stevens

The Bishop of Leicester

In the busy-ness of my life as a bishop, I need to have times when I can go to my place of prayer, gradually relax myself and wait on God. Sometimes my mind goes racing on with its plans, as if I was God planning everything. Yet sometimes I enter a great reservoir of stillness and silence and I come to realise that God can be the source and inspirer of all our work if we will only stop playing God ourselves.

Psalm 51:6

You desire truth in the inward being;
therefore teach me wisdom in my secret heart.
(NRSV)

THE RT. REVD DR JAMES JONES

THE BISHOP OF LIVERPOOL

My favourite Bible verse changes from year to year. At the moment this is my favourite. The liberating thing about being loved by God is to know that you can be utterly truthful before him. He knows everything about us. There is nothing that we can or should hide from him. And even though he knows everything about us, he still loves us. I once heard someone say that if you could devise a camera that could photograph our thoughts, none of us would have a friend in the world! God sees us as we really are and he loves us. Being able to be truthful before him means being able to be truthful with ourselves about ourselves. When we see those stains on our life we can be truthful even about those because his love extends to forgiving us completely and washing us clean. That is why Jesus, the Saviour of the world, who died to take away our sins, is such good news.

Psalm 91

He that dwelleth in the secret place of the most High shall abide under the shadow of the Almighty.

I will say of the Lord, He is my refuge and my fortress: my God; in him will I trust.

Surely he shall deliver thee from the snare of the fowler, and from the noisome pestilence.

He shall cover thee with his feathers, and under his wings shalt thou trust: his truth shall be thy shield and buckler.

Thou shalt not be afraid for the terror by night; nor for the arrow that flieth by day;

Nor for the pestilence that walketh in darkness; nor for the destruction that wasteth at noonday.

A thousand shall fall at thy side, and ten thousand at thy right hand; but it shall not come nigh thee.

Only with thine eyes shalt thou behold and see the reward of the wicked.

Because thou hast made the Lord, which is my refuge, even the most High, thy habitation;

There shall no evil befall thee, neither shall any plague come nigh thy dwelling.

For he shall give his angels charge over thee, to keep thee in all thy ways.

They shall bear thee up in their hands, lest thou dash thy foot against a stone.

Thou shalt tread upon the lion and adder: the young lion and the dragon shalt thou trample under feet.

Because he hath set his love upon me, therefore will I deliver him: I will set him on high, because he hath known my name.

He shall call upon me, and I will answer him: I will be with him in trouble; I will deliver him, and honour him.

With long life will I satisfy him, and shew him my salvation. (AV)

PAUL JONES

MUSICIAN AND ENTERTAINER

This is an amazing psalm of protection. God wants his children safe. This shows his wonderful love towards us.

Psalm 104:10–23

You make springs gush forth in the valleys;
they flow between the hills,
giving drink to every wild animal;
the wild asses quench their thirst.
By the streams the birds of the air have their habitation;
they sing among the branches.
From your lofty abode you water the mountains;
the earth is satisfied with the fruit of your work.

You cause the grass to grow for the cattle,
and plants for people to use,
To bring forth food from the earth,
and wine to gladden the human heart,
oil to make the face shine,
and bread to strengthen the human heart.
The trees of the LORD are watered abundantly,
the cedars of Lebanon that he planted.
In them the birds build their nests;
the stork has its home in the fir trees.
The high mountains are for the wild goats;
the rocks are a refuge for the coneys.
You have made the moon to mark the seasons;
the sun knows its time for setting.
You make darkness, and it is night,
when all the animals of the forest come creeping out.
The young lions roar for their prey,
seeking their food from God.
When the sun rises, they withdraw
and lie down in their dens.
People go out to their work
and to their labour until the evening. (NRSV)

Julian Marcus

Retired Headteacher and Worker for Christian Aid

This is part of the lovely creation hymn from Psalm 104, possibly composed in its original version in the fourteenth century BC during the reign of Pharaoh Akhenaton. It seems to me to be a celebration of the beauty of nature, but this is no idealised picture – the poet is well aware that the lions at night will hunt and kill. The poem places human beings in the context of the natural world and shows a delight in its fruits: bread, olive oil, wine and water. It speaks also of the dignity of work. Thus it is for me not only beautiful, but also a 'text' for our times in our stewardship of the natural world and our quest for a just society.

Psalm 118:24

This is the day which the Lord hath made; we will rejoice and be glad in it. (AV)

The Rt. Revd Robert Hardy

The Bishop of Lincoln

I once heard an elderly bishop preach on this text when, as a young curate, I took boys camping on the Isle of Man. I love it because it is positive and I try to live by it.

Psalm 121

I will lift up mine eyes unto the hills, from whence cometh my help.

My help cometh from the Lord, which made heaven and earth.

He will not suffer thy foot to be moved: he that keepeth thee will not slumber.

Behold, he that keepeth Israel shall neither slumber nor sleep.

The Lord is thy keeper: the Lord is thy shade upon thy right hand.

The sun shall not smite thee by day, nor the moon by night.

The Lord shall preserve thee from all evil: he shall preserve thy soul.

The Lord shall preserve thy going out and thy coming in from this time forth, and even for evermore. (AV)

The Rt. Hon. William Hague, MP
Former Leader of the Conservative Party
It is uplifting and moving and a psalm that fills me with inspiration.

Rosamunde Pilcher
Writer
There is always comfort in being out of doors, a sense of continuance and the varied beauties of nature. Also a renewed sense of proportion, so that trivialities sink to their own size.

Psalm 128:2

For thou shalt eat the labour of thine hands: happy shalt thou be, and it shall be well with thee. (AV)

RON MOODY
ACTOR AND NOVELIST
Nothing is really worth having unless you have earned it yourself. Gifts are nice, but in this respect the happiest is the giver. By the same token, gambling is destructive and huge winnings on the lottery are a social disgrace. Mind you, with a wife and six children, I wouldn't exactly give it back. (But I'd still rather earn it.)

❧

Psalm 130:3–4

If you, Lord, should keep account of sins,
who could hold his ground?
But with you is forgiveness,
so that you may be revered. (REB)

The Revd Eric Allen
Former United Reformed Church Moderator, Mersey Province

It is central to my faith. God's forgiveness is the greatest gift for my life and for humankind, for 'all have sinned and fall short of the glory of God' (Romans 3:23). God's forgiveness evokes reverence and fear, not complacency and carelessness. There is forgiveness with him – not to do as I like, thinking 'God will forgive, that's his job', but to respond to God's free unmerited gift by living responsibly.

This Psalm 130 and St Paul's letter to the Romans changed the life of Martin Luther (see his hymn 'Out of the depths . . . rejoice and sing', in the translation of Richard Massie).

~

Psalm 131

O Lord, my heart is not proud,
  nor are my eyes haughty;
I do not busy myself with great matters
  or things too marvellous for me.
No; I submit myself, I account myself lowly,
  as a weaned child clinging to its mother.
O Israel, look for the Lord
  now and evermore. (NEB)

Rabbi Lionel Blue
Writer and Broadcaster
I sometimes say it late at night in bed and it helps me go to sleep.

Psalm 137:1

By the rivers of Babylon, there we sat down, yea, we wept, when we remembered Zion. (AV)

RUTH RENDELL

AUTHOR

Though it is very short, it seems to me to contain the whole anguish of those taken or driven from their homes and exiled to a strange land. There are many other verses I love but this one speaks to me most powerfully and it comes into my mind when I hear or read of people seeking asylum or immigrating to this country, perhaps in great fear. I think of it, too, when I remember times of happiness gone by.

Psalm 139:1–18

O LORD, thou hast searched me, and known me.

Thou knowest my down-sitting and mine uprising, thou understandest my thought afar off.

Thou compassest my path and my lying down, and art acquainted with all my ways.

For there is not a word in my tongue, but lo, O LORD, thou knowest it altogether.

Thou hast beset me behind and before, and laid thine hand upon me.

Such knowledge is too wonderful for me; it is high, I cannot attain unto it.

Whither shall I go from thy spirit? Or whither shall I flee from thy presence?

If I ascend up into heaven, thou art there: if I make my bed in hell, behold, thou art there.

If I take the wings of the morning, and dwell in the uttermost parts of the sea;

Even there shall thy hand lead me, and thy right hand shall hold me.

If I say, Surely the darkness shall cover me; even the night shall be light about me.

Yea, the darkness hideth not from thee; but the night shineth as the day: the darkness and the light are both alike to thee.

For thou has possessed my reins: thou hast covered me in my mother's womb.

I will praise thee; for I am fearfully and wonderfully made: marvellous are thy works; and that my soul knoweth right well.

My substance was not hid from thee, when I was made in secret, and curiously wrought in the lowest parts of the earth.

Thine eyes did see my substance, yet being unperfect; and in thy book all my members were written, which in continuance were fashioned, when as yet there was none of them.

How precious also are thy thoughts unto me, O God! How great is the sum of them!

If I should count them, they are more in number than the sand: when I awake, I am still with thee. (AV)

Sir Mark Moody-Stuart

Chairman of Royal Dutch/Shell, 1997–2001

It was my father's favourite and I remember him reading it to us as children. We sang it at our wedding thirty-seven years ago and I would like it at my funeral! It is an awesome yet comforting acknowledgment of God's omniscience and omnipresence.

Psalm 144:1–2

Blessed be the LORD my strength, which teacheth my hands to war, and my fingers to fight.

My goodness, and my fortress; my high tower, and my deliverer; my shield, and he in whom I trust; who subdueth my people under me. (AV)

LAVINIA BYRNE
WRITER AND BROADCASTER
These verses speak to me of the power and strength of God who is an advocate of those who stand in need of protection. They remind me that ultimate authority lies with the transcendent God.

~

Psalm 144:12

That our daughters may be as corner stones, polished after the similitude of a palace. (AV)

The Lady Patience Baden-Powell

Vice President of the Girl Guides Association, 1990–2000

The motto of the Anglican convent where I was at school in Bulawayo, Zimbabwe, was 'That our daughters may be as the polished corners of the temple'. This is something rather wonderful to try and live up to and worth trying. I mostly fail.

Psalm 150

Praise ye the Lord. Praise God in his sanctuary: praise him in the firmament of his power.

Praise him for his mighty acts: praise him according to his excellent greatness.

Praise him with the sound of the trumpet: praise him with the psaltery and harp.

Praise him with the timbrel and dance: praise him with stringed instruments and organs.

Praise him upon the loud cymbals: praise him upon the high sounding cymbals.

Let every thing that hath breath praise the Lord. Praise ye the Lord. (AV)

Dulcie Gray (Mrs Michael Denison)

Actress and Writer

It is such a happy psalm, so full of faith and good temper. It praises God in the 'firmament of his power'. And God among all the galaxies in the heavens, is the God of all creation, and worthy of all praise.

Proverbs 3:5–6

Trust in the Lord with all your heart
and lean not on your own understanding;
in all your ways acknowledge him,
and he will make your paths straight. (NIV)

Dr Stephanie Cook, BM, B.Ch., MA
Athlete and Doctor
Modern Pentathlon Olympic Gold Medallist
It provides me with a reminder that the Lord is in control of my life and that he has a plan for me to follow so it is important for me to look to him first in everything that I do and endeavour to keep him at the centre of my life.

~

Proverbs 4:7

Wisdom is the principal thing; therefore get wisdom: and with all thy getting get understanding. (AV)

Anne Fine
Author
I do not think it is any accident that it is in marble over so many of our great public libraries.

~

Proverbs 6:10–11

A little sleep, a little slumber,
a little folding of the hands to rest,
and poverty will come upon you like a vagabond,
and want like an armed man. (RSV)

GYLES BRANDRETH
WRITER AND BROADCASTER
I have these verses framed above my desk and they keep my nose to the grindstone.

Proverbs 28:1

The wicked flee when no man pursueth: but the righteous are bold as a lion. (AV)

Dick Francis
Author
I have chosen this verse as it reflects my philosophy in life – be honest, have courage and be loyal to those who deserve it.

~

Proverbs 31:10–31

Who can find a virtuous woman? for her price is far above rubies.

The heart of her husband doth safely trust in her, so that he shall have no need of spoil.

She will do him good and not evil all the days of her life.

She seeketh wool, and flax, and worketh willingly with her hands.

She is like the merchants' ships; she bringeth her food from afar.

She riseth also while it is yet night, and giveth meat to her household, and a portion to her maidens.

She considereth a field, and buyeth it; with the fruit of her hands she planteth a vineyard.

She girdeth her loins with strength, and strengtheneth her arms.

She perceiveth that her merchandise is good: her candle goeth not out by night.

She layeth her hands to the spindle, and her hands hold the distaff.

She stretcheth out her hand to the poor; yea, she reacheth forth her hands to the needy.

She is not afraid of the snow for her household: for all her household are clothed with scarlet.

She maketh herself coverings of tapestry; her clothing is silk and purple.

Her husband is known in the gates, when he sitteth among the elders of the land.

She maketh fine linen, and selleth it; and delivereth girdles unto the merchant.

Strength and honour are her clothing; and she shall rejoice in time to come.

She openeth her mouth with wisdom; and in her tongue is the law of kindness.

She looketh well to the ways of her household, and eateth not the bread of idleness.

Her children arise up, and call her blessed; her husband also, and he praiseth her.

Many daughters have done virtuously, but thou excellest them all.

Favour is deceitful, and beauty is vain; but a woman that feareth the Lord, she shall be praised.

Give her of the fruit of her hands; and let her own works praise her in the gates. (AV)

Jonathan Cecil

Actor and Writer

My wife and marriage are the greatest gifts God has given me. If any feminist should object to the passage, I would say that it is a beautiful description of any good, selfless person, regardless of sex.

Ecclesiastes 1:4–9

A generation goes, and a generation comes,
  but the earth remains for ever.
The sun rises and the sun goes down,
  and hastens to the place where it rises.
The wind blows to the south,
  and goes round to the north;
round and round goes the wind,
  and on its circuits the wind returns.
All streams run to the sea,
  but the sea is not full;
to the place where the streams flow,
  there they flow again.
All things are full of weariness;
  a man cannot utter it;
the eye is not satisfied with seeing,
  nor the ear filled with hearing.
What has been is what will be,
  and what has been done is what will be done;
  and there is nothing new under the sun. (RSV)

Joanna Lumley

Actress

It seems to echo one of the great true sayings – what goes around, comes around – 'there is nothing new under the sun' is a magnificent sentence!

Ecclesiastes 3:1–15

To every thing there is a season, and a time to every purpose under the heaven:

A time to be born, and a time to die; a time to plant, and a time to pluck up that which is planted;

A time to kill, and a time to heal; a time to break down, and a time to build up:

A time to weep, and a time to laugh; a time to mourn, and a time to dance;

A time to cast away stones, and a time to gather stones together; a time to embrace, and a time to refrain from embracing;

A time to get, and a time to lose; a time to keep, and a time to cast away;

A time to rend, and a time to sew; a time to keep silence, and a time to speak;

A time to love, and a time to hate; a time of war, and a time of peace.

What profit hath he that worketh in that wherein he laboureth?

I have seen the travail, which God hath given to the sons of men to be exercised in it.

He hath made every thing beautiful in his time: also he hath set the world in their heart, so that no man can find out the work that God maketh from the beginning to the end.

I know that there is no good in them, but for a man to rejoice, and to do good in his life.

And also that every man should eat and drink, and enjoy the good of all his labour, it is the gift of God.

I know that, whatsoever God doeth, it shall be for ever: nothing can be put to it, nor any thing taken from it: and God doeth it, that men should fear before him.

That which hath been is now; and that which is to be hath already been; and God requireth that which is past. (AV)

Richard Briers

Actor

I chose this passage because it is so beautifully written and so profound.

Sue Cook

Broadcaster

It makes me stand back and recognise that there is a time and place for all actions and feelings. You will experience all these emotions and experiences in your life. Don't be anxious about it. It is the natural order of things. I first became aware of this passage through a song called 'Turn, Turn, turn' recorded by a group called the Byrds in the 1960s.

John Craven

Broadcaster

From a young child, this has always been a favourite because it is so easy to understand and so complete – a perfect explanation of the impact that God has on all of us. I particularly like verse 14: 'I know that whatever God does endures for ever: nothing can be added to it, nor anything taken from it; God has made it so, in order that men should fear before him' (RSV).

Edwina Currie

Author

The verses from Ecclesiastes seem to me to represent a balanced life. There are times when you feel very down; when you've lost someone dear, or when fate seems to be dealing you a very poor hand. But things will improve. There's a pattern to be found behind the ups and downs of life. So cheer up! Make the most of where you are.

Anna Ford
Broadcaster and Journalist

It is an example of the timeless wisdom of parts of the Bible.

Lord Nigel Lawson
Former Chancellor of the Exchequer and Speaker

It combines sublime poetry with profound truth.

Eric Nicoli
Chairman of the EMI Group plc

I like it because it is true and it offers a perspective on life as we know it.

Paula Wilcox
Actress

Verse 1 expresses a deep philosophical truth in beautiful language.

~

Ecclesiastes 3:1, 8

There is a season for everything, a time for every occupation under heaven . . .
A time for war,
A time for peace. (JB)

General Sir Charles Guthrie, GCB, LVO, OBE, ADC

General Chief of the Defence Staff, 1997–2001

This text constantly reminds me that there is nothing new under the sun. All my adult life I have lived with the tension of war and peace. I have strived and longed for peace while preparing for war. Peace is the gift from God and war is often the human response. These verses encourage me – even from the Old Testament times, God understands just how humanity works. His word encourages, challenges and rewards us. So, there is nothing new under the sun and God is the one constant on which we can rely.

~

Ecclesiastes 9:10

Whatsoever thy hand findeth to do, do it with thy might; for there is no work, nor device, nor knowledge, nor wisdom, in the grave, whither thou goest. (AV)

LORD MARSHALL

CHAIRMAN OF BRITISH AIRWAYS

It is a constant reminder to me that personal fulfilment in this life comes from grasping opportunity with commitment and responsibility.

~

Ecclesiastes 9:11–12

I returned, and saw under the sun, that the race is not to the swift, nor the battle to the strong, neither yet bread to the wise, nor yet riches to men of understanding, nor yet favour to men of skill; but time and chance happeneth to them all.

For man also knoweth not his time: as the fishes that are taken in an evil net, and as the birds that are caught in the snare; so are the sons of men snared in an evil time, when it falleth suddenly upon them. (AV)

Huw Edwards
Presenter of Six O'clock News
I like these verses because they offer hope to all who struggle in life. They offer inspiration to the weak and the disadvantaged. They provide a healthy outlook on life for all of us.

These verses were also chosen by
The Rt. Hon. David Trimble, MP, MLA
First Minister of Northern Ireland and Nobel Peace Prize Laureate

Ecclesiastes 11:1, 2, 5; 12:1, 2, 8, 13–14

Cast thy bread upon the waters: for thou shalt find it after many days.

Give a portion to seven, and also to eight; for thou knowest not what evil shall be upon the earth . . .

As thou knowest not what is the way of the spirit, nor how the bones do grow in the womb of her that is with child: even so thou knowest not the works of God who maketh all . . .

Remember now thy Creator in the days of thy youth, while the evil days come not, nor the years draw nigh, when thou shalt say, I have no pleasure in them;

While the sun, or the light, or the moon, or the stars, be not darkened, nor the clouds return after the rain . . .

Vanity of vanities, saith the preacher; all is vanity . . .

Let us hear the conclusion of the whole matter: Fear God, and keep his commandments: for this is the whole duty of man.

For God shall bring every work into judgment, with every secret thing, whether it be good, or whether it be evil. (AV)

Martin Bell, OBE

Former MP and Journalist

Ecclesiastes 12:1 reminds us of the things that matter rather than those that are ephemeral. And that when we are young it is not too early to start thinking about them.

Sir Iain Vallance

Former Chairman of BT plc

I have chosen Ecclesiastes 12:1–2 because these verses capture the superb poetry of the Old Testament.

Richard Whiteley

Presenter of Countdown

These are two very poetic and emotive chapters. The language is momentous and evocative. They were read by the headmaster at Giggleswick School at the end of each term in chapel. The service was held in the dark except for two candles on the altar. Many boys and staff were in tears.

~

Song of Solomon 2:8–14

The voice of my beloved! Behold, he cometh leaping upon the mountains, skipping upon the hills.

My beloved is like a roe or a young hart: behold, he standeth behind our wall, he looketh forth at the windows, shewing himself through the lattice.

My beloved spake, and said unto me, Rise up, my love, my fair one, and come away.

For lo, the winter is past, the rain is over and gone;

The flowers appear on the earth; the time of the singing of birds is come, and the voice of the turtle is heard in our land;

The fig tree putteth forth her green figs, and the vines with the tender grape give a good smell. Arise, my love, my fair one, and come away.

O my dove, that art in the clefts of the rock, in the secret places of the stairs, let me see thy countenance, let me hear thy voice; for sweet is thy voice, and thy countenance is comely. (AV)

Joan Bakewell

Broadcaster

It is one of the greatest love songs ever written. Also when I was at school, part of it – 'For lo the winter is past' – was set as the school anthem.

Stuart Hall

Broadcaster

I have selected verses 11 and 12 because of their optimism; light replaces dark, beauty shines through. It is a message of simple happiness, of hope – apposite in these times of base commercialism and break-up of true values.

Song of Solomon 5:10–6:3

My beloved is white and ruddy, the chiefest among ten thousand.

His head is as the most fine gold, his locks are bushy, and black as a raven.

His eyes are as the eyes of doves by the rivers of waters, washed with milk, and fitly set.

His cheeks are as a bed of spices, as sweet flowers: his lips are like lilies, dropping sweet smelling myrrh.

His hands are as gold rings set with the beryl: his belly is as bright ivory overlaid with sapphires.

His legs are as pillars of marble, set upon sockets of fine gold: his countenance is as Lebanon, excellent as the cedars.

His mouth is most sweet: yea, he is altogether lovely. This is my beloved and this is my friend, O daughters of Jerusalem.

Whither is thy beloved gone, O thou fairest among women? whither is thy beloved turned aside? that we may seek him with thee.

My beloved is gone down into his garden, to the beds of spices, to feed in the gardens, and to gather lilies.

I am my beloved's, and my beloved is mine: he feedeth among the lilies. (AV)

Stephanie Cole

Actress

We so often forget to celebrate being physical beings, the sensuality of being alive, the savouring of the moments and this is a reminder.

Isaiah 1:11–17

To what purpose is the multitude of your sacrifices unto me? saith the Lord: I am full of the burnt offerings of rams, and the fat of fed beasts; and I delight not in the blood of bullocks, or of lambs, or of he goats.

When ye come to appear before me, who hath required this at your hand, to tread my courts?

Bring no more vain oblations; incense is an abomination unto me; the new moons and sabbaths, the calling of assemblies, I cannot away with; it is iniquity, even the solemn meeting.

Your new moons and your appointed feasts my soul hateth: they are a trouble unto me; I am weary to bear them.

And when ye spread forth your hands, I will hide mine eyes from you: yea, when ye make many prayers, I will not hear: your hands are full of blood.

Wash you, make you clean; put away the evil of your doings from before mine eyes: cease to do evil.

Learn to do well; seek judgment, relieve the oppressed, judge the fatherless, plead for the widow. (AV)

Rabbi Julia Neuberger

Chief Executive of the King's Fund

It teaches us that ritual is not enough, and the semblance of religion. What is needed is good deeds, and an awareness of those less fortunate than oneself, and one's obligation to them.

Isaiah 24:4–7; 55:12–13

The earth mourns and withers,
the world languishes and withers;
the heavens languish together with the earth.
The earth lies polluted
under its inhabitants;
for they have transgressed the laws, violated the statutes,
broken the everlasting covenant.
Therefore a curse devours the earth,
and its inhabitants suffer for their guilt;
therefore the inhabitants of the earth are scorched,
and few men are left.
The wine mourns,
the vine languishes,
all the merry-hearted sigh . . .

For you shall go out in joy,
and be led forth in peace;
the mountains and the hills before you
shall break forth into singing,
and all the trees of the field shall clap their hands.
Instead of the thorn shall come up the cypress;
instead of the briar shall come up the myrtle;
and it shall be to the Lord for a memorial,
for an everlasting sign which shall not be cut off.
(RSV)

The Rt. Hon. Lord Paddy Ashdown of Norton-Sub-Hamdon, KBE

Former Leader of the Liberal Democrats

These verses remind us of our duty of stewardship of the earth.

❧

Isaiah 30:30

And the Lord shall cause his glorious voice to be heard, and shall shew the lighting down of his arm, with the indignation of his anger, and with the flame of a devouring fire, with scattering, and tempest, and hailstones. (AV)

Bill Giles, OBE

Former Head of BBC Weather Centre

An illustration of God's power and judgment on men by bringing heavy storms of thunder and hail, which was one of the ten plagues of Egypt as described in Exodus.

Isaiah 32:17

And the work of righteousness shall be peace; and the effect of righteousness quietness and assurance for ever. (AV)

Joel Edwards

General Director of the Evangelical Alliance

Many of us think of righteousness, either in abstract theological terms, or in moral terms. Righteousness includes both. But here, Isaiah offers us something tangible with which to relate our personal holiness, the character of God and our everyday situations, which come to test us. It is peace and quiet confidence.

~

Isaiah 40:3–4

The voice of him that crieth in the wilderness, Prepare ye the way of the Lord, make straight in the desert a highway for our God.

Every valley shall be exalted, and every mountain and hill shall be made low: and the crooked shall be made straight, and the rough places plain. (AV)

John McCarthy
Writer and Broadcaster
I find the imagery so powerful in this passage. The idea of vast physical obstacles like mountains being flattened by thought is tremendously exciting. I have no great faith but was moved by this passage at a time in my life when everything seemed 'crooked' and uncertain. I needed majestic language like this.

Isaiah 40:21–31

Have you not known? Have you not heard?
  Has it not been told you from the beginning?
  Have you not understood from the foundations of the
    earth?
It is he who sits above the circle of the earth,
  and its inhabitants are like grasshoppers;
who stretches out the heavens like a curtain,
  and spreads them like a tent to live in:
who brings princes to naught;
  and makes the rulers of the earth as nothing.

Scarcely are they planted, scarcely sown,
  scarcely has their stem taken root in the earth,
when he blows upon them, and they wither,
  and the tempest carries them off like stubble.

To whom then will you compare me,
  or who is my equal? says the Holy One.
Lift up your eyes on high and see:
  Who created these?
He who brings out their host and numbers them,
  calling them all by name;
because he is great in strength,
  mighty in power,
  not one is missing.

Why do you say, O Jacob,
  And speak, O Israel,
My way is hidden from the Lord,
  and my right is disregarded by my God?
Have you not known? Have you not heard?

The Lord is the everlasting God,
the Creator of the ends of the earth.
He does not faint or grow weary;
his understanding is unsearchable.
He gives power to the faint,
and strengthens the powerless.
Even youths will faint and be weary;
and the young will fall exhausted;
but those who wait for the Lord shall renew their strength,
they shall mount up with wings like eagles,
they shall run and not be weary,
they shall walk and not faint. (NRSV)

The Rt. Revd George Cassidy

The Bishop of Southwell

Verse 31 reminds me of the priority of prayer, 'Wait on the Lord' reminds me of the promise of God's renewal.

Dr Stephanie Cook, BM, B.Ch., MA

Athlete and Doctor

Modern Pentathlon Olympic Gold Medallist

Verse 31 gives me renewed energy and reminds me that my strength comes not from myself but from God, and with his help I can do more than I ever imagined possible.

The Rt. Revd Dr Wilfred Wood, KA

The Bishop of Croydon

The passage speaks so eloquently of the grandeur, majesty and mercy of God, which makes his love for us human beings all the more awe-inspiring.

Isaiah 41:10

Fear not, for I am with you,
  be not dismayed, for I am your God;
I will strengthen you, I will help you,
  I will uphold you with my victorious right hand.
  (RSV)

The late Sir Harry Secombe, CBE
Presenter, Singer and Comedian
Sir Harry wrote this a few months before he died:

This verse has comforted me in my present difficulty and I am sure will inspire others.

~

Isaiah 43:1–5

But now, thus says Yahweh,
who created you, Jacob,
who formed you, Israel:

Do not be afraid, for I have redeemed you;
I have called you by your name, you are mine.
Should you pass through the sea, I will be with you;
or through rivers, they will not swallow you up.
Should you walk through fire, you will not be
scorched
and the flames will not burn you.
For I am Yahweh, your God,
the Holy One of Israel, your saviour.

I give Egypt for your ransom,
and exchange Cush and Seba for you.
Because you are precious in my eyes,
because you are honoured and I love you,
I give men in exchange for you,
peoples in return for your life.
Do not be afraid, for I am with you. (JB)

Jonathan Aitken
Theology Student, Oxford University

These verses speak to me of the strength and security that faith in God offers even in the worst of life's troubles and turmoils. Throughout a long saga of dramatic difficulties in my own life, which included a prison sentence, I found that these verses were a great source of reassurance. Isaiah's message is that the power of God's redeeming love can bring the faithful believer unharmed through even the worst disaster the world can inflict.

The Rt. Revd Jack Nicholls

The Bishop of Sheffield

My spiritual director, Mother Mary Claire, chose verse 1 as her confirmation text and passed it to me.

Isaiah 52:7–8; 53:1–12

How beautiful upon the mountains are the feet of him that bringeth good tidings, that publisheth peace; that bringeth good tidings of good, that publisheth salvation; that saith unto Zion, Thy God reigneth!

Thy watchmen shall lift up the voice; with the voice together shall they sing: for they shall see eye to eye, when the Lord shall bring again Zion . . .

Who hath believed our report? and to whom is the arm of the Lord revealed?

For he shall grow up before him as a tender plant, and as a root out of a dry ground: he hath no form nor comeliness; and when we shall see him, there is no beauty that we should desire him.

He is despised and rejected of men; a man of sorrows, and acquainted with grief: and we hid as it were our faces from him; he was despised and we esteemed him not.

Surely he hath borne our griefs, and carried our sorrows: yet we did esteem him stricken, smitten of God, and afflicted.

But he was wounded for our transgressions, he was bruised for our iniquities: the chastisement of our peace was upon him; and with his stripes we are healed.

All we like sheep have gone astray; we have turned every one to his own way; and the Lord hath laid on him the iniquity of us all.

He was oppressed, and he was afflicted, yet he opened not his mouth: he is brought as a lamb to the slaughter, and as a sheep before her shearers is dumb, so he openeth not his mouth.

He was taken from prison and from judgment: and who

shall declare his generation? for he was cut off out of the land of the living: for the transgression of my people was he stricken.

And he made his grave with the wicked, and with the rich in his death; because he had done no violence, neither was any deceit in his mouth.

Yet it pleased the Lord to bruise him; he hath put him to grief: when thou shalt make his soul an offering for sin, he shall see his seed, he shall prolong his days, and the pleasure of the Lord shall prosper in his hand.

He shall see of the travail of his soul, and shall be satisfied: by his knowledge shall my righteous servant justify many: for he shall bear their iniquities.

Therefore will I divide him a portion with the great, and he shall divide the spoil with the strong; because he hath poured out his soul unto death: and he was numbered with the transgressors; and he bare the sin of many, and made intercession for the transgressors. (AV)

Prunella Scales

Actress

I knew it well as a child as it was often read in school prayers. Also it forms a good part of Handel's *Messiah*, which we performed with the neighbouring boys' school.

Helen Shapiro

Singer

Written 700 years before Jesus, Isaiah 53 speaks prophetically about him – the Messiah – who would come and bear the sins of all of us upon himself; being the once-and-for-all sacrifice for sin; the atonement; the Redeemer. I committed my life to him in 1987.

~

Jeremiah 1:4–10

The word of Yahweh was addressed to me, saying,
'Before I formed you in the womb I knew you;
before you came to birth I consecrated you;
I have appointed you as prophet to the nations'.

I said, 'Ah, Lord Yahweh; look, I do not know how to speak:
I am a child!'
But Yahweh replied,
'Do not say, "I am a child".
Go now to those to whom I send you
and say whatever I command you.
Do not be afraid of them,
for I am with you to protect you –
it is Yahweh who speaks!'

Then Yahweh put out his hand and touched my mouth and
said to me:
'There! I am putting my words into your mouth.
Look, today I am setting you
over nations and over kingdoms,
to tear up and to knock down,
to destroy and to overthrow,
to build and to plant.' (JB)

The Rt. Revd John Gladwin
The Bishop of Guildford
Jeremiah is a hero of mine. This is his call as a young person. It shows a deep love of God.

The Rt. Revd Peter Price

The Bishop of Kingston

Verse 5 reminds me that God has loved me, and loves each of us, from the moment of our conception until our dying day, and calls us all to live as if we were loved people, to speak out for justice and to live our lives in hope.

Jeremiah 29:11–14

'For I know the plans I have for you,' declares the Lord, 'plans to prosper you and not to harm you, plans to give you hope and a future. Then you will call upon me and come and pray to me, and I will listen to you. You will seek me and find me when you seek me with all your heart. I will be found by you,' declares the Lord, 'and will bring you back from captivity. I will gather you from all the nations and places where I have banished you,' declares the Lord, 'and will bring you back to the place from which I carried you into exile.' (NIV)

Wayne Jacobs

Professional Football Player

It shows us how much God wants a relationship with us, to bless us, to guide us, to protect us, to be all things to us, to be our loving Father. But as in any relationship it's a two-way thing and the main ingredient has to be our heart and, as we give ourselves over to him, he helps us to fulfil the life he has for us.

Ezekiel 1:1–14

Now it came to pass in the thirtieth year, in the fourth month, in the fifth day of the month; as I was among the captives by the river of Chebar, that the heavens were opened, and I saw visions of God.

In the fifth day of the month, which was the fifth year of king Jehoiachin's captivity,

The word of the Lord came expressly unto Ezekiel the priest, the son of Buzi, in the land of the Chaldeans by the river Chebar; and the hand of the Lord was there upon him.

And I looked, and, behold, a whirlwind came out of the north, a great cloud, and a fire unfolding itself, and a brightness was about it, and out of the midst thereof as the colour of amber, out of the midst of the fire.

Also out of the midst thereof came the likeness of four living creatures. And this was their appearance; they had the likeness of a man.

And every one had four faces, and every one had four wings.

And their feet were straight feet; and the sole of their feet was like the sole of a calf's foot: and they sparkled like the colour of burnished brass.

And they had the hands of a man under their wings on their four sides; and they four had their faces and their wings.

Their wings were joined one to another; they turned not when they went; they went every one straight forward.

As for the likeness of their faces, they four had the face of a man, and the face of a lion, on the right side: and they four had the face of an ox on the left side; they four also had the face of an eagle.

Thus were their faces: and their wings were stretched

upward; two wings of every one were joined one to another, and two covered their bodies.

And they went every one straight forward: whither the spirit was to go, they went; and they turned not when they went.

As for the likeness of the living creatures, their appearance was like burning coals of fire, and like the appearance of lamps: it went up and down among the living creatures; and the fire was bright, and out of the fire went forth lightning.

And the living creatures ran and returned as the appearance of a flash of lightning. (AV)

The Rt. Revd Dr Kenneth Stevenson

The Bishop of Portsmouth

Ezekiel is my favourite Old Testament prophet. The reason for this particular passage being my favourite is that it forms the opening vision for Ezekiel, with the four living creatures and the chariot – a vision of perpetual movement and stillness at the same time, and of the presence of God in heaven and on earth.

~

Amos 5:21–24

I hate, I despise your feast days, and I will not smell in your solemn assemblies.

Though ye offer me burnt offerings and your meat offerings, I will not accept them: neither will I regard the peace offerings of your fat beasts.

Take thou away from me the noise of thy songs: for I will not hear the melody of thy viols.

But let judgment run down as waters, and righteousness as a mighty stream. (AV)

The Revd Martin Camroux
United Reformed Church Minister at Trinity Church, Sutton, Surrey
The Times *Preacher of the Year 2001*
The great insight of the prophets was that to know God is to do justice. It is this insight which gives biblical religion its great moral force. Today when the Church is frequently tempted to run away from radical political involvement in favour of inward-looking pietism it is a profound reminder that without a commitment to the poor, biblical religion has lost its essential nature.

The Revd Paul Newman
Chaplain at Her Majesty's Prison, Downview
The prophetic message of Amos reminds us that prayer, praise and worship must be met by active compassion and justice.

Jonah 4:11

And should not I spare Nineveh, that great city, wherein are more than sixscore thousand persons that cannot discern between their right hand and their left hand; and also much cattle? (AV)

Rabbi Lionel Blue

Writer and Broadcaster

It is the only book which ends with an unanswered question, and I'm curious about Jonah's reply and if it got him out of the sulks. Also there's humour in it and irony and therapy.

Micah 6:8

He hath shewed thee, O man, what is good; and what doth the Lord require of thee, but to do justly, and to love mercy, and to walk humbly with thy God? (AV)

Baroness P. D. James of Holland Park, OBE

Writer

I have loved this verse since childhood and have found it a guide to living.

THE APOCRYPHA

1 Esdras 3:10–12

The first wrote, Wine is the strongest.
The second wrote, The king is strongest.
The third wrote, Women are strongest: but above all things Truth beareth away the victory. (AV)

SYLVIA SYMS
ACTRESS
The reason I chose this verse is because it's precise, simple and curiously witty.

~

Tobit 12:7

It is good to keep close the secret of a king, but it is honourable to reveal the works of God. Do that which is good, and no evil shall touch you. (AV)

Lord William Waldegrave of North Hill

Former Politician, now Banker

The reason I chose this verse is first because I love the story of Tobit, Tobias and the angel. Second, because the story contains the only pet dog I know in the Bible. Third, because the verse is a good summary of the duties owed by a politician to his or her earthly masters, and to God.

❧

Ecclesiasticus, or the Wisdom of Jesus Son of Sirach 32:3

Speak, thou that art the elder, for it becometh thee, but with sound judgment; and hinder not musick. (AV)

Colin Davis

Musician and Principal Conductor of the London Symphony Orchestra

The music? Music at table, literally. Also the unheard music, which is the order of the universe, of the earth and of man's heart and to which too few listen.

THE NEW TESTAMENT

❧

Matthew 5:3–11

Blessed are the poor in spirit: for theirs is the kingdom of heaven.
Blessed are they that mourn: for they shall be comforted.
Blessed are the meek: for they shall inherit the earth.
Blessed are they which do hunger and thirst after righteousness: for they shall be filled.
Blessed are the merciful: for they shall obtain mercy.
Blessed are the pure in heart: for they shall see God.
Blessed are the peacemakers: for they shall be called the children of God.
Blessed are they which are persecuted for righteousness' sake: for theirs is the kingdom of heaven.
Blessed are ye, when men shall revile you, and persecute you, and shall say all manner of evil against you falsely, for my sake. (AV)

THE RT. HON. MICHAEL ANCRAM, QC, MP
SHADOW FOREIGN SECRETARY AND DEPUTY LEADER OF THE CONSERVATIVE PARTY
I believe these verses summarise the Christian message.

MICHAEL ASPEL
BROADCASTER
Verse 8 was written on a sampler over the bed I occupied as an evacuee in Somerset in World War Two. It represents an innocence which, sadly, has gone from my life.

The Rt. Hon. Tony Benn
MP for Chesterfield, 1984–2001
The passage says it all.

Barbara Dickson
Singer and Actress
These verses encompass everything one needs to know.

Robert Powell
Actor
The Sermon on the Mount speaks for itself.

The Rt. Hon. John Redwood, MP
The Sermon on the Mount encapsulates so much Christian wisdom, and is uplifting during life's trials.

The Rt. Hon. Clare Short, MP
My favourite part of the Bible is the Sermon on the Mount because it shows that Jesus stood for social justice for all, especially the poor. If all Christians stood by this, the world would be a better place.

❧

Matthew 5:14–16

Ye are the light of the world. A city that is set on an hill cannot be hid.

Neither do men light a candle, and put it under a bushel, but on a candlestick; and it giveth light unto all that are in the house.

Let your light so shine before men, that they may see your good works, and glorify your Father which is in heaven. (AV)

Dominic Kirwan
Singer
The reason I like this Scripture is that it talks about living our lives in such a way that the Lord shines through and that we can share with others his love and desire for us to live.

~

Matthew 5:43–45

Ye have heard that it hath been said, Thou shalt love thy neighbour, and hate thine enemy.

But I say unto you, Love your enemies, bless them that curse you, do good to them that hate you, and pray for them which despitefully use you, and persecute you;

That ye may be the children of your Father which is in heaven, for he maketh his sun to rise on the evil and on the good, and sendeth rain on the just and on the unjust. (AV)

George Baker

Actor and Writer

It seems to me to sum up a philosophy of life which we should struggle to attain but which is almost impossible. However, I believe it is very important at least to try.

Matthew 6:9–13

After this manner therefore pray ye: Our Father which art in heaven, Hallowed be thy name.

Thy kingdom come. Thy will be done in earth, as it is in heaven.

Give us this day our daily bread.

And forgive us our debts, as we forgive our debtors.

And lead us not into temptation, but deliver us from evil: For thine is the kingdom, and the power, and the glory, for ever. Amen. (AV)

MELVYN BRAGG

WRITER, BROADCASTER AND PRESENTER

This and Psalm 23 are my favourite passages because the long usage, beautiful language and the comfort of the words themselves have become fixed in my mind as something of a refuge.

Matthew 6:25–27

Therefore I tell you, do not worry about your life, what you will eat or drink; or about your body, what you will wear. Is not life more important than food, and the body more important than clothes? Look at the birds of the air; they do not sow or reap or store away in barns, and yet your heavenly Father feeds them. Are you not much more valuable than they? Who of you by worrying can add a single hour to his life? (NIV)

The Revd Geoffrey Gleed

Personnel and Training Manager, and Resident Chaplain at the Blunsdon House Hotel, near Swindon, Wiltshire

Way back in 1979 I was told by my GP that I was suffering from anxiety/stress. Then, one afternoon, my Bible fell open at the reading from Matthew's Gospel where Jesus is teaching about worry and it was verse 27 that really hit me between the eyes, 'Who of you by worrying can add a single hour to his life?' For the first time in ages a passage from the Bible came to life for me. One thing became clear: worry had damaged my health both physically and mentally and had reduced my ability to trust myself, let alone have faith in God.

My worries came because I was trying to juggle far too many things in my life. I wrote endless 'to do' lists and even wrote down things I had already done, so that I could cross them off straight away and feel good.

I now imagine that everything I have to deal with is contained in separate musical boxes, each playing a different tune. When I open just one box at a time, I will hear the tune very clearly. If I open too many boxes at one time, all I will hear is a cacophony of sound which creates tension, anxiety and stress. It was these words of Jesus that began to make me think this way.

~

Matthew 6:28–29

And why take ye thought for raiment? Consider the lilies of the field, how they grow; they toil not, neither do they spin:

And yet I say unto you, That even Solomon in all his glory was not arrayed like one of these. (AV)

David Bellamy

Presenter and Botanist

The message encapsulated in this verse from the Bible has made me what I am, for though cast in God's image humanity must be humble before creation.

Jilly Cooper

Novelist

It may encourage one to be a bit idle and passive, but it does stop you worrying and I adore wild flowers.

Alan Titchmarsh

Presenter and Author

I chose this passage for fairly obvious reasons.

Matthew 7:1–2

Judge not, that ye be not judged.

For with what judgment ye judge, ye shall be judged: and with what measure ye mete, it shall be measured to you again. (AV)

John Junkin
Actor
It reminds us that none of us are perfect and a little understanding makes all our journeys a little easier.

Matthew 7:7–8

Ask, and it shall be given you; seek and ye shall find; knock, and it shall be opened unto you:

For every one that asketh receiveth; and he that seeketh findeth; and to him that knocketh it shall be opened. (AV)

Russell Boulter

Actor

Christianity is not passive, it is a dynamic relationship with Almighty God as your heavenly Father. This is a promise from Jesus that God will respond if you want him to.

Maggie Philbin

TV Presenter

It encourages us to be brave enough to ask for help, advice and guidance when we need it. I think it's great to remember these words in every aspect of life. People are usually keen to help and so often we are too shy or too afraid to ask for things, which others would be very happy and flattered to give.

~

Matthew 7:12

Do for others what you want them to do for you. (GNB)

Peter Alliss

Golf Presenter

I have a very simplistic view of all things religious and I have always thought this passage sums up the whole thing in a nutshell and would do as a guideline for anyone anywhere in the world.

Gareth Jones

Executive Director, Abbey National plc

I think this passage is a good philosophy to rule behaviour.

~

Matthew 10:16–39

I am sending you out like sheep among wolves. Therefore be as shrewd as snakes and as innocent as doves.

Be on your guard against men; they will hand you over to the local councils and flog you in their synagogues. On my account you will be brought before governors and kings as witnesses to them and to the Gentiles. But when they arrest you, do not worry about what to say or how to say it. At that time you will be given what to say, for it will not be you speaking, but the Spirit of your Father speaking through you.

Brother will betray brother to death, and a father his child; children will rebel against their parents and have them put to death. All men will hate you because of me, but he who stands firm to the end will be saved. When you are persecuted in one place, flee to another. I tell you the truth, you will not finish going through the cities of Israel before the Son of Man comes.

A student is not above his teacher, nor a servant above his master. It is enough for the student to be like his teacher, and the servant like his master. If the head of the house has been called Beelzebub, how much more the members of his household!

So do not be afraid of them. There is nothing concealed that will not be disclosed, or hidden that will not be made known. What I tell you in the dark, speak in the daylight; what is whispered in your ear, proclaim from the roofs. Do not be afraid of those who kill the body but cannot kill the soul. Rather, be afraid of the One who can destroy both soul and body in hell. Are not two sparrows sold for a penny? Yet not one of them will fall to the ground apart from the will of your Father. And even the very hairs of your head are all numbered. So don't be afraid; you are worth more than many sparrows.

Whoever acknowledges me before men, I will also acknowledge him before my Father in heaven. But whoever disowns me before men, I will disown him before my Father in heaven.

Do not suppose that I have come to bring peace to the earth. I did not come to bring peace, but a sword. For I have come to turn

'a man against his father,
  a daughter against her mother,
a daughter-in-law against her mother-in-law –
  a man's enemies will be the members of his own household.'

Anyone who loves his father or mother more than me is not worthy of me; anyone who loves his son or daughter more than me is not worthy of me; and anyone who does not take his cross and follow me is not worthy of me. Whoever finds his life will lose it, and whoever loses his life for my sake will find it. (NIV)

CARO FRASER

AUTHOR

I first read this passage in the Gideon Bible given to me as a child. The sentiments contained in these verses, spoken by Jesus to his disciples, are extraordinarily challenging. They conjure up a notion of Jesus as a fiery orator, a man of passionate principles and ruthless dedication, neither peaceful nor gentle, as we usually think of him, but utterly uncompromising. The verses, while inspiring, are a reminder of how great the demands of dedication to God can be.

Matthew 11:25–30

At that time Jesus answered and said, I thank thee, O Father, Lord of heaven and earth, because thou hast hid these things from the wise and prudent, and hast revealed them unto babes.

Even so, Father; for so it seemed good in thy sight.

All things are delivered unto me of my Father: and no man knoweth the Son, but the Father; neither knoweth any man the Father, save the Son, and he to whomsoever the Son will reveal him.

Come unto me, all ye that labour and are heavy laden, and I will give you rest.

Take my yoke upon you, and learn of me; for I am meek and lowly in heart: and ye shall find rest unto your souls.

For my yoke is easy, and my burden is light. (AV)

The Rt. Revd William Ind

The Bishop of Truro

My experience of the Christian faith has been that I have learned much more from people who have a simple understanding of faith than from those who have a rather intellectual, clever understanding. One of the dimensions of this passage which I think most of us miss is that the father/son image in it is concerned not just with a family relationship but also with the idea of the son being the father's apprentice and I find the idea of Jesus learning the father's trade is a very good one, not least because of course it then passes on to us that we too are apprentices in the school of the gospel. The last couple of verses, 28 to 30, are, I think, a great encouragement to people who carry heavy burdens.

Christopher Martin-Jenkins

Cricket Correspondent and Commentator

I have chosen verses 28 to 30 because I have found it to be true. Someone once told me that we should imagine lobbing any worries or fears to Jesus who will catch them as softly as if one had tossed him an orange. I find that a helpful image, being used to throwing cricket balls and to trying to land golf balls softly by the pin!

Paula Tilbrook

Actress

Verses 28 to 30 are the words that I have repeated when I have been at my darkest hour, and it has indeed given me peace.

Matthew 16:24–28

Then said Jesus unto his disciples, If any man will come after me, let him deny himself, and take up his cross, and follow me.

For whosoever will save his life shall lose it: and whosoever will lose his life for my sake shall find it.

For what is a man profited, if he shall gain the whole world, and lose his own soul? or what shall a man give in exchange for his soul?

For the Son of man shall come in the glory of his Father with his angels; and then he shall reward every man according to his works.

Verily I say unto you, There be some standing here, which shall not taste of death, till they see the Son of man coming in his kingdom. (AV)

Cliff Michelmore

Retired Broadcaster

I once heard an inspirational sermon on these verses preached by Dr Donald Soper (a marvellous Methodist preacher and leader). These verses are one of the great challenges to any Christian. To leave self behind – to follow. 'Come with me,' He said. How many of us can truly say, 'I will'?

Matthew 19:13–15

Then were there brought unto him little children, that he should put his hands on them, and pray: and the disciples rebuked them.

But Jesus said, Suffer little children, and forbid them not, to come unto me: for of such is the kingdom of heaven.

And he laid his hands on them, and departed thence. (AV)

Mollie Sugden
Actress
I subscribe to the NSPCC. I cannot think of anything more appalling than cruelty to children and babies.

❧

Matthew 25:29

For unto every one that hath shall be given, and he shall have abundance: but from him that hath not shall be taken away even that which he hath. (AV)

Robert Goddard

Novelist

I call it to mind frequently. I puzzle over its real meaning. I observe its truth and I note the strangeness of that truth.

Matthew 25:31–46

When the Son of man shall come in his glory, and all the holy angels with him, then shall he sit upon the throne of his glory:

And before him shall be gathered all nations: and he shall separate them one from another, as a shepherd divideth his sheep from the goats:

And he shall set the sheep on his right hand, but the goats on the left.

Then shall the King say unto them on his right hand, Come, ye blessed of my Father, inherit the kingdom prepared for you from the foundation of the world:

For I was an hungred, and ye gave me meat: I was thirsty, and ye gave me drink: I was a stranger and ye took me in:

Naked, and ye clothed me: I was sick, and ye visited me: I was in prison, and ye came unto me.

Then shall the righteous answer him, saying, Lord, when saw we thee an hungred, and fed thee? or thirsty, and gave thee drink?

When saw we thee a stranger, and took thee in? or naked, and clothed thee?

Or when saw we thee sick, or in prison, and came unto thee?

And the King shall answer and say unto them, Verily I say unto you, inasmuch as ye have done it unto one of the least of these my brethren, ye have done it unto me.

Then shall he say also unto them on the left hand, Depart from me, ye cursed, into everlasting fire, prepared for the devil and his angels:

For I was an hungred, and ye gave me no meat: I was thirsty, and ye gave me no drink:

I was a stranger, and ye took me not in: naked, and ye

clothed me not: sick, and in prison, and ye visited me not.

Then shall they also answer him, saying, Lord, when saw we thee an hungred, or athirst, or a stranger, or naked, or sick, or in prison, and did not minister unto thee?

Then shall he answer them, saying Verily I say unto you, Inasmuch as ye did it not to one of the least of these, ye did it not to me.

And these shall go away into everlasting punishment: but the righteous into life eternal. (AV)

The Revd Thomas Johns

Acting Chaplain General, HM Prison Service

Verse 36: It is hard to understand that Jesus lives within the prisons of our land; but chaplains and Christian volunteers who frequent the inside of our gaols will not hesitate to say that in an extraordinary way they came across Jesus in prison and they left the prison feeling better than when they went in.

The Revd Ruth Scott

Priest, Writer and Broadcaster

I chose this passage, not because I think it poetic or because I believe in damnation – I don't. I've chosen it because it says that those who enter into the kingdom of heaven are not necessarily those who believe the right things about Jesus, but those who live with humanity. It's such an inclusive passage that cuts through every barrier that our inhumanity erects. It doesn't matter what is your faith, creed, colour or gender. All that concerns God is the way you care for other human beings, particularly those in need. That is the core of my own faith.

THE RT. HON. SIR DAVID STEEL, KBE, MSP

FORMER LEADER OF THE LIBERAL PARTY

This passage is Christ's compelling parable, illustrating 'Love thy neighbour as thyself'.

❧

Matthew 28:20

And, lo, I am with you alway, even unto the end of the world. Amen. (AV)

Deborah Grant

Actress

The comfort and knowledge that Jesus is with me always – no matter what happens – I am never alone.

Geoffrey Wheeler

Broadcaster

I have chosen this passage because it means that we are never alone. Never ever. We all of us go through times when we feel so alone, times when nothing seems to go right. And there are times when we feel we deserve to be because we have done things we know we should not have done. But whether we feel defeated or ashamed, sad or lonely, the one great fact remains: we are never alone. The Lord is with us, close by, ready to hear us and help us, if only we will ask. It is the most wonderful, comforting, cheering thought. And it is true. We prove it when we ask. But if we don't then we may never know.

Mark 4:13–22, 30–32

And he said unto him, Know ye not this parable? And how then will ye know all parables?

The sower soweth the word.

And these are they by the way side, where the word is sown; but when they have heard, Satan cometh immediately, and taketh away the word that was sown in their hearts.

And these are they likewise which are sown on stony ground; who, when they have heard the word, immediately receive it with gladness;

And have no root in themselves, and so endure but for a time: afterward, when affliction or persecution ariseth for the word's sake, immediately they are offended.

And these are they which are sown among thorns; such as hear the word,

And the cares of this world, and the deceitfulness of riches, and the lusts of other things entering in, choke the word, and it becometh unfruitful.

And these are they which are sown on good ground; such as hear the word, and receive it, and bring forth fruit, some thirtyfold, some sixty, and some an hundred.

And he said unto them, Is a candle brought to be put under a bushel, or under a bed? and not to be set on a candlestick?

For there is nothing hid, which shall not be manifested; neither was any thing kept secret, but that it should come abroad . . .

And he said, Whereunto shall we liken the kingdom of God? or with what comparison shall we compare it?

It is like a grain of mustard seed, which, when it is sown in the earth, is less than all the seeds that be in the earth:

But when it is sown, it groweth up, and becometh greater

than all herbs, and shooteth out great branches; so that the fowls of the air may lodge under the shadow of it. (AV)

The Rt. Hon. Tony Blair, MP

The Prime Minister

In a letter from 10 Downing Street, a communication officer for Mr Blair said that he enjoys the verses in Mark 4.

Mark 4:37–41

And there arose a great storm of wind, and the waves beat into the ship, so that it was now full.

And he was in the hinder part of the ship, asleep on a pillow: and they awake him, and say unto him, Master, carest thou not that we perish?

And he arose, and rebuked the wind, and said unto the sea, Peace, be still. And the wind ceased, and there was a great calm.

And he said unto them, Why are ye so fearful? how is it that ye have no faith?

And they feared exceedingly, and said one to another, What manner of man is this, that even the wind and the sea obey him? (AV)

Admiral Sir Michael Boyce, GCB, OBE, ADC

First Sea Lord and Chief of Naval Staff, 1998–2001; Chief of the Defence Staff, 2001–

I have been in some frightening weather conditions at sea. On each occasion, I recall the story of Jesus calming the storm, and have always found it a great comfort; the awesome power of the sea, tempered by the reassurance that God is ultimately in control of it.

Mark 8:34–37

And when he had called the people unto him with his disciples also, he said unto them, Whosoever will come after me, let him deny himself, and take up his cross, and follow me.

For whosoever will save his life shall lose it; but whosoever shall lose his life for my sake and the gospel's, the same shall save it.

For what shall it profit a man, if he shall gain the whole world, and lose his own soul?

Or what shall a man give in exchange for his soul? (AV)

The Rt. Revd Barry Rogerson
The Bishop of Bristol
I believe these are the essence of Christian living and the gospel we preach.

Mark 12:31

And the second is like, namely this, Thou shalt love thy neighbour as thyself. There is none other commandment greater than these. (AV)

Crispin Blunt, MP

If you have this injunction permanently in mind you can't go far wrong. It is the central tenet of Christian philosophy, which can be followed without requiring belief in God or that a carpenter's son in Palestine 2,000 years ago was the Son of God. If we can be true to this verse our behaviour is likely to be to the benefit of all, including ourselves.

~

Luke 1:41

And it came to pass, that, when Elisabeth heard the salutation of Mary, the babe leaped in her womb; and Elisabeth was filled with the Holy Ghost. (AV)

Professor the Lord David Alton of Liverpool

Director of the Foundation for Citizenship, Liverpool John Moores University

The reason I love this is because it reminds me that the first person to greet Jesus was an unborn child, and St Luke alone among the Gospel writers records this special moment. He was, of course, a doctor and would have been formed in the Hellenistic codes of medicine, with great reverence to the unborn child and the sanctity of human life.

~

Luke 1:46–55

And Mary said,
'My soul magnifies the Lord,
and my spirit rejoices in God my Saviour,
for he has regarded the low estate of his handmaiden.
For behold, henceforth all generations will call me
blessed;
for he who is mighty has done great things for me,
and holy is his name.
And his mercy is on those who fear him
from generation to generation.
He has shown strength with his arm,
he has scattered the proud in the imagination of their
hearts,
he has put down the mighty from their thrones,
and exalted those of low degree;
he has filled the hungry with good things,
and the rich he has sent empty away.
He has helped his servant Israel,
in remembrance of his mercy,
as he spoke to our fathers,
to Abraham and to his posterity for ever.' (RSV)

Cherie Booth, QC

Barrister

My favourite passage in the Bible is the Magnificat, a beautiful part of St Luke's Gospel. It is the words Mary spoke when visiting her kinswoman Elizabeth after she learnt that she was pregnant.

~

Luke 2:25–32

And, behold, there was a man in Jerusalem, whose name was Simeon; and the same man was just and devout, waiting for the consolation of Israel: and the Holy Ghost was upon him.

And it was revealed unto him by the Holy Ghost, that he should not see death, before he had seen the Lord's Christ.

And he came by the Spirit into the temple: and when the parents brought in the child Jesus, to do for him after the custom of the law,

Then took he him up in his arms, and blessed God, and said,

Lord, now lettest thou thy servant depart in peace, according to thy word:

For mine eyes have seen thy salvation,

Which thou hast prepared before the face of all people;

A light to lighten the Gentiles, and the glory of thy people Israel. (AV)

Anton Rogers

Actor

This is the Nunc Dimittis, or the Song of Simeon, which forms part of Evening Prayer. I love the wording and it reminds me of the beautiful Evensong service; in context, Simeon had been told that he would not see death before he had seen the Lord's Christ. When Jesus was brought into the Temple, Simeon took him in his arms, blessed God and said, 'Lord, now lettest thou thy servant depart in peace . . .' These lovely words epitomise for me the glory of God and the hope of salvation. Words for me, particularly in my profession as an actor, have huge significance.

~

Luke 5:4

Now when he had left speaking, he said unto Simon, Launch out into the deep and let down your nets for a draught. (AV)

The Rt. Hon. John Gummer, MP
It challenges us all to go out there and do what needs to be done, secure in God's love. He expects us to 'launch out into the deep' and not to stay safe at home while others seize the opportunities and challenges.

Luke 5:17–26

And it came to pass on a certain day, as he was teaching, that there were Pharisees and doctors of the law sitting by, which were come out of every town of Galilee, and Judaea, and Jerusalem: and the power of the Lord was present to heal them.

And, behold, men brought in a bed a man which was taken with a palsy: and they sought means to bring him in, and to lay him before him.

And when they could not find by what way they might bring him in because of the multitude, they went upon the housetop, and let him down through the tiling with his couch into the midst before Jesus.

And when he saw their faith, he said unto him, Man, thy sins are forgiven thee.

And the scribes and the Pharisees began to reason, saying, Who is this which speaketh blasphemies? Who can forgive sins, but God alone?

But when Jesus perceived their thoughts, he answering said unto them, What reason ye in your hearts?

Whether is easier, to say, Thy sins be forgiven thee; or to say, Rise up and walk?

But that ye may know that the Son of man hath power upon earth to forgive sins, (he said unto the sick of the palsy,) I say unto thee, Arise, and take up thy couch, and go into thine house.

And immediately he rose up before them, and took up that whereon he lay, and departed to his own house, glorifying God.

And they were all amazed, and they glorified God, and were filled with fear, saying, We have seen strange things today. (AV)

The Rt. Hon. Sir Brian Mawhinney, Ph.D., MP

The Christian faith is built on a personal relationship with Jesus Christ, though often people see it more in ethical or behavioural terms. My biblical understanding is that Christians are not people who are superior, better living or the most religious and pious people. Christians are those whose sins have been forgiven and that is the joyous message of the passage in Luke.

~

Luke 7:47–48

'And so, I tell you, her great love proves that her many sins have been forgiven; where little has been forgiven, little love is shown.' Then he said to her, 'Your sins are forgiven.' (NEB)

The Rt. Hon. Virginia Bottomley, MP
Most of us in the pews are at times bad, mad or sad but still welcomed.

Luke 10:25–37

And, behold, a certain lawyer stood up, and tempted him, saying, Master, what shall I do to inherit eternal life?

He said unto him, What is written in the law? how readest thou?

And he answering said, Thou shalt love the Lord thy God with all thy heart, and with all thy soul, and with all thy strength, and with all thy mind; and thy neighbour as thyself.

And he said unto him, Thou hast answered right: this do, and thou shalt live.

But he, willing to justify himself, said unto Jesus, And who is my neighbour?

And Jesus answering said, A certain man went down from Jerusalem to Jericho, and fell among thieves, which stripped him of his raiment, and wounded him, and departed, leaving him half dead.

And by chance there came down a certain priest that way: and when he saw him he passed by on the other side.

And likewise a Levite, when he was at the place, came and looked on him, and passed by on the other side.

But a certain Samaritan, as he journeyed, came where he was: and when he saw him, he had compassion on him.

And went to him, and bound up his wounds, pouring in oil and wine, and set him on his own beast, and brought him to an inn, and took care of him.

And on the morrow when he departed, he took out two pence, and gave them to the host, and said unto him, Take care of him; and whatsoever thou spendest more, when I come again, I will repay thee.

Which now of these three, thinkest thou, was neighbour unto him that fell among the thieves?

And he said, He that shewed mercy on him. Then said Jesus unto him, Go and do thou likewise. (AV)

The Revd Robert Ellis

Minister, Southernhay and St Thomas United Reformed Church, Exeter, Devon

I have chosen verse 27 because, like the apostle Paul, I believe that love is the greatest of all qualities, deriving as it does from the nature of God. For me, Love is the quality that gives true meaning to life . . . the quality that makes life worthwhile and worth living . . . the quality that should motivate all we are and all we do.

This verse, in a few words, summarises for me what my Christian discipleship demands. I believe I am called upon not only to love God, but to love like God, generously and graciously, unselfishly and unconditionally, without favour, without limit and without expectation of response. Needless to say, I fail miserably, but what a challenge!

Frederick Forsyth

Author

This passage illustrates the virtues of charity, compassion and generosity, not necessarily to a close friend, but to a complete stranger, even one from a different part of the world.

Rt. Hon. The Lord Irvine of Lairg

The Lord Chancellor

I was brought up in the Church of Scotland where the reading of the Scriptures plays a central role in worship. My lifelong favourite has been the Good Samaritan. It teaches so many lessons.

First it shows that kindness can come from the most unexpected quarter. While the self-righteous of their day, the priest and the Levite passed by on the other side and ignored the plight of their fellow man, a semi-pagan and despised foreigner showed that he knew more about the love of God than the outwardly devout leaders of religion.

But the parable also teaches the value of education. Without the wherewithal to pay for the victim's care, the Samaritan's good intentions could not be turned to account. But, by using his training to earn his living, he is able to help those who have fallen on hard times. Education is to be seen not solely as a means of self-advancement: it is a means of acquiring financial independence the better to discharge our obligations to society.

Above all Jesus makes clear that the lawyer who provoked the parable with the question 'and who is my neighbour?', was asking the wrong question. Jesus teaches that the proper question is 'To whom can I be a neighbour?' and the answer is 'To anyone whose need constitutes a claim on my love'. It is neighbourliness, not neighbourhood, that makes a neighbour. This applies to our leaders as it does to each one of us in our daily lives.

Canon Roger Royle

Broadcaster, Writer and Priest

Verse 33 explains to me exactly the mission of Jesus Christ. He was born into this world so as to come where people are, both as individuals and as society as a whole. He is there to meet our real needs.

Luke 10:38–42

As Jesus and his disciples were on their way, he came to a village where a woman named Martha opened her home to him. She had a sister called Mary, who sat at the Lord's feet listening to what he said. But Martha was distracted by all the preparations that had to be made. She came to him and asked, 'Lord, don't you care that my sister has left me to do the work by myself? Tell her to help me!'

'Martha, Martha,' the Lord answered, 'you are worried and upset about many things, but only one thing is needed. Mary has chosen what is better, and it will not be taken away from her.' (NIV)

Victoria Glendinning
Author

The reason I chose this passage is because I think Jesus was too hard on Martha. Someone always has to get the dinner. It makes me want to argue.

~

Luke 12:13–34

A man in the crowd said to Jesus, 'Teacher, tell my brother to divide with me the property our father left us.'

Jesus answered him, 'My friend, who gave me the right to judge or to divide the property between you two?' And he went on to say to them all, 'Watch out and guard yourselves from every kind of greed; because a person's true life is not made up of the things he owns, no matter how rich he may be.'

Then Jesus told them this parable: 'There was once a rich man who had land which bore good crops. He began to think to himself, "I haven't anywhere to keep all my crops. What can I do? This is what I will do," he told himself; "I will tear down my barns and build bigger ones, where I will store my corn and all my other goods. Then I will say to myself, Lucky man! You have all the good things you need for many years. Take life easy, eat, drink, and enjoy yourself!" But God said to him, "You fool! This very night you will have to give up your life; then who will get all these things you have kept for yourself?" '

And Jesus concluded, 'This is how it is with those who pile up riches for themselves but are not rich in God's sight.'

Then Jesus said to the disciples, 'And so I tell you not to worry about the food you need to stay alive or about the clothes you need for your body. Life is much more important than food, and the body much more important than clothes. Look at the crows: they don't sow seeds or gather a harvest; they don't have store-rooms or barns; God feeds them! You are worth so much more than birds! Can any of you live a bit longer by worrying about it? If you can't manage even such a small thing, why worry about the other things? Look how the wild flowers grow: they don't work or make clothes for themselves. But I tell you that not even King Solomon with all his wealth had clothes as beautiful as one of these flowers. It is God who clothes the wild grass – grass that is here today and gone tomorrow, burnt up in the oven. Won't he be all the more sure to clothe you? How little faith you have!

'So don't be all upset, always concerned about what you will eat and drink. (For the pagans of this world are always concerned about all these things.) Your Father knows that you need these things. Instead, be concerned with his Kingdom, and he will provide you with these things.

'Do not be afraid, little flock, for your Father is pleased to give you the Kingdom. Sell all your belongings and give the money to the poor. Provide for yourselves purses that don't wear out, and save your riches in heaven, where they will never decrease, because no thief can get to them, and no moth can destroy them. For your heart will always be where your riches are.' (GNB)

Julian Pettifer

Broadcaster

Its advice has never been more relevant and timely.

Luke 12:35–37

Let your loins be girded about, and your lights burning;

And ye yourselves like unto men that wait for their lord, when he will return from the wedding; that when he cometh and knocketh, they may open unto him immediately.

Blessed are those servants, whom the lord when he cometh shall find watching: verily I say unto you, that he shall gird himself, and make them to sit down to meat, and will come forth and serve them. (AV)

The Revd Baroness Kathleen Richardson of Calow, OBE

Member of the House of Lords and Methodist Minister

We often think of the Christian faith as offering service to others. It is, in this short parable of Jesus, also seen as being willing to receive what God gives.

Luke 15:10–32

Likewise, I say unto you, there is joy in the presence of the angels of God over one sinner that repenteth.

And he said, A certain man had two sons:

And the younger of them said to his father, Father, give me the portion of goods that falleth to me. And he divided unto them his living.

And not many days after the younger son gathered all together, and took his journey into a far country, and there wasted his substance with riotous living.

And when he had spent all, there arose a mighty famine in that land; and he began to be in want.

And he went and joined himself to a citizen of that country; and he sent him into his fields to feed swine.

And he would fain have filled his belly with the husks that the swine did eat: and no man gave unto him.

And when he came to himself, he said, How many hired servants of my father's have bread enough and to spare, and I perish with hunger!

I will arise and go to my father, and will say unto him, Father, I have sinned against heaven, and before thee,

And am no more worthy to be called thy son: make me as one of thy hired servants.

And he arose, and came to his father. But when he was yet a great way off, his father saw him, and had compassion, and ran, and fell on his neck, and kissed him.

And the son said unto him, Father, I have sinned against heaven, and in thy sight, and am no more worthy to be called thy son.

But the father said to his servants, Bring forth the best robe, and put it on him; and put a ring on his hand, and shoes on his feet.

And bring hither the fatted calf, and kill it; and let us eat, and be merry:

For this my son was dead, and is alive again; he was lost, and is found. And they began to be merry.

Now his elder son was in the field: and as he came and drew nigh to the house, he heard music and dancing.

And he called one of the servants, and asked what these things meant.

And he said unto him, Thy brother is come; and thy father hath killed the fatted calf, because he hath received him safe and sound.

And he was angry, and would not go in: therefore came his father out, and intreated him.

And he answering said to his father, Lo, these many years do I serve thee, neither transgressed I at any time thy commandment: and yet thou never gavest me a kid, that I might make merry with my friends:

But as soon as this thy son was come, which hath devoured thy living with harlots, thou hast killed for him the fatted calf.

And he said unto him, Son, thou art ever with me, and all that I have is thine.

It was meet that we should make merry, and be glad: for this thy brother was dead, and is alive again; and was lost, and is found. (AV)

Dickie Bird, MBE

Cricket Test Umpire

I have many favourite verses in the Bible but to pick just one I will choose verse 20 of the story of the Prodigal Son. This story speaks to me of the freely forgiving love of the Father for errant mankind.

THE REVD JONATHAN JENNINGS

PRESS SECRETARY TO THE ARCHBISHOP OF CANTERBURY

It is so full of surprises – the story never ends the way you think it will. It should have been a morality tale of how the faithful son was rewarded while the wasted son ended up with the pigs. But it didn't end there . . . and that's the real lesson for us all.

CHRIS PATTEN

EUROPEAN COMMISSIONER

The parable of the Prodigal Son reminds us of the most important – and perhaps most difficult – attributes of any Christian or for that matter, decent human being of any faith: generosity of spirit.

SIMON THOMAS

BLUE PETER *PRESENTER*

Apart from it being a great story, it is a great insight into God and how much he loves us. To me it means a lot. During my life there have been times when I have made a mess of things, been selfish and self-centred, and have ignored God and what he knows is best for my life. Sometimes I have felt that I have made such a mess of things that there is no way God could ever, or would ever, forgive me for what I have done. The story of the Lost Son is a source of real encouragement for me, because I know that however much I may constantly make mistakes, God will always forgive me and welcome me back with open arms, like the father did with his son.

Luke 23:42–43

Then he said, 'Jesus, remember me when you come into your kingdom.' He replied, 'Truly I tell you, today you will be with me in Paradise.' (NRSV)

Richard Baker, OBE

Broadcaster and Writer

It's very touching, showing the trust of the condemned criminal and the love and forgiveness of Jesus.

The Rt. Revd James Lawton Thompson

The Bishop of Bath and Wells

I love the fact that Christ in the middle of his own suffering turns to the penitent offender on the cross next to him and promises him paradise. I believe profoundly in this love of Christ for offenders including me, and trust his word that there is a dimension of God described as paradise.

Luke 24:13–31

And, behold, two of them went that same day to a village called Emmaus, which was from Jerusalem about threescore furlongs.

And they talked together of all these things which had happened.

And it came to pass, that, while they communed together and reasoned, Jesus himself drew near, and went with them.

But their eyes were holden that they should not know him.

And he said unto them, What manner of communications are these that ye have one to another, as ye walk, and are sad?

And the one of them, whose name was Cleopas, answering said unto him, Art thou only a stranger in Jerusalem, and hast not known the things which are come to pass there in these days?

And he said unto them, What things? And they said unto him, Concerning Jesus of Nazareth, which was a prophet mighty in deed and word before God and all the people:

And how the chief priests and our rulers delivered him to be condemned to death, and have crucified him.

But we trusted that it had been he which should have redeemed Israel: and beside all this, to day is the third day since these things were done.

Yea, and certain women also of our company made us astonished, which were early at the sepulchre;

And when they found not his body, they came, saying, that they had also seen a vision of angels, which said that he was alive.

And certain of them which were with us went to the

sepulchre, and found it even so as the women had said: but him they saw not.

Then he said unto them, O fools, and slow of heart to believe all that the prophets have spoken:

Ought not Christ to have suffered these things, and to enter into his glory?

And beginning at Moses and all the prophets, he expounded unto them in all the scriptures the things concerning himself.

And they drew nigh unto the village, whither they went: and he made as though he would have gone further. But they constrained him, saying, Abide with us: for it is toward evening, and the day is far spent. And he went in to tarry with them.

And it came to pass, as he sat at meat with them, he took bread, and blessed it, and brake, and gave to them.

And their eyes were opened, and they knew him; and he vanished out of their sight. (AV)

THE RT. REVD DR DAVID STANCLIFFE

THE BISHOP OF SALISBURY

This narrative encapsulates the four key stages of growth in the Christian life which are rehearsed each time we celebrate the Eucharist.

1 Meeting together and starting a conversation (Gathering of the Community).
2 Setting our story alongside the story of what God has done for his people (Liturgy of the Word).
3 Engagement leading to transformation – offering us an experience of change (Liturgy of the Sacrament – breaking of bread).
4 Sending us out with a renewed sense of purpose to share what we have become (Dismissal Rite).

Luke 24:28

As they came near the village to which they were going, he walked ahead as if he were going on. (NRSV)

The Revd Margaret Engler
Chaplain at Her Majesty's Prison, Highdown
It is reassuring that God does not stay where he is not invited; that he gives us the chance to invite him to wait with us after the initial introduction. He does not swamp us, nor coerce, nor compel us to remain with him; it is through our invitation to him, freely given, that we get to know him better. A verse which sums up, for me, the concepts of free will and choice.

~

John 1:1–14

In the beginning was the Word, and the Word was with God, and the Word was God.

The same was in the beginning with God.

All things were made by him; and without him was not any thing made that was made.

In him was life; and the life was the light of men.

And the light shineth in darkness, and the darkness comprehended it not.

There was a man sent from God, whose name was John.

The same came for a witness, to bear witness of the Light, that all men through him might believe.

He was not that Light, but was sent to bear witness of that Light.

That was the true Light, which lighteth every man that cometh into the world.

He was in the world, and the world was made by him, and the world knew him not.

He came unto his own, and his own received him not.

But as many as received him, to them gave he power to become the sons of God, even to them that believe on his name:

Which were born, not of blood, nor of the will of the flesh, nor of the will of man, but of God.

And the Word was made flesh, and dwelt among us, (and we beheld his glory, the glory as of the only begotten of the Father,) full of grace and truth. (AV)

The Revd Steve Chalke

Baptist Minister and Founding Director of Oasis Trust

Verse 14 has always been (and continues to be) a source of inspiration, motivation and challenge. I particularly try to focus on the fact that Jesus isn't only full of *truth*, but is also full of *grace*.

The Revd Dr David Cornick

General Secretary of the United Reformed Church

Verse 14 is the very heart of the good news of the gospel, that God (the word, the intent, thought and being of God) became part of the human story in Jesus from Nazareth, accessible to us in the shape and time of a life. History holds no greater treasure than this. Small wonder that angels sang, shepherds came and kings knelt.

Jonathan Dimbleby

Writer and Broadcaster

Verses 1 to 5 are beautiful and simple. The idea is beautiful and complex. The meaning is abstract but universal. You do not have to be a Christian to find illumination here.

Nigel Havers

Actor

The reason I have selected this passage is first from school, but mainly because all actors need 'the Word' which is why a script is known as the 'Bible'.

Patricia Hodge

Actress

'In the beginning was the Word' – I have always felt this to be so appropriate for my profession because without the art of the writer no theatre can exist. I am eternally sorry that our writers are not given more importance in this country.

The Rt. Revd Dr Michael Nazir-Ali

The Bishop of Rochester

I have chosen verses 1 to 5 because they are read at the Christmas Midnight Mass. It reminds us that God loved the world so much that he sent his Word, Jesus, to save the world he created. This Word is the source of all life and lightens everyone in the world. Although darkness, through the cross, tried to extinguish the Light of the World, the resurrection shows us that love and light will always prevail.

The Rt. Revd David Smith

The Bishop of Bradford

The more I meditate on verse 14, the more riches I discover.

John 1:39

He saith unto them, Come and see. (AV)

Nick Butterworth

Author and Illustrator

Two disciples of John the Baptist ask Jesus where he is staying. Jesus answers (verse 39), 'Come and see.' On the face of it, there is nothing remarkable here. It's a simple answer to a simple question. But, to me, the very simplicity is what *is* remarkable. There is no hint of celebrity guardedness. No 'mind your own business'. Nor is there any attempt to use the question as an opportunity to preach or teach. Jesus says, 'Come and see.' He is friendly. He has time for these two men. In fact they are invited to stay because it is late afternoon.

I would love to have been able to eavesdrop on their conversation. Did they discuss the meaning of life or maybe a good short-cut through Jerusalem avoiding the market . . . ? Or both?

A pity I wasn't there. So I'll just have to have my own conversation with him instead.

John 3:1–15

Now there was a man of the Pharisees, named Nicodemus, a ruler of the Jews. This man came to Jesus by night and said to him, 'Rabbi, we know that you are a teacher come from God; for no one can do these signs that you do, unless God is with him.' Jesus answered him, 'Truly, truly, I say to you, unless one is born anew, he cannot see the kingdom of God.' Nicodemus said to him, 'How can a man be born when he is old? Can he enter a second time into his mother's womb and be born?' Jesus answered, 'Truly, truly, I say to you, unless one is born of water and the Spirit, he cannot enter the kingdom of God. That which is born of the flesh is flesh, and that which is born of the Spirit is spirit. Do not marvel that I said to you, "You must be born anew." The wind blows where it wills, and you hear the sound of it, but you do not know whence it comes or whither it goes; so it is with every one who is born of the Spirit.' Nicodemus said to him, 'How can this be?' Jesus answered him, 'Are you a teacher of Israel, and yet you do not understand this? Truly, truly, I say to you, we speak of what we know, and bear witness to what we have seen; but you do not receive our testimony. If I have told you earthly things and you do not believe, how can you believe if I tell you heavenly things? No one has ascended into heaven but he who descended from heaven, the Son of man. And as Moses lifted up the serpent in the wilderness, so must the Son of man be lifted up, that whoever believes in him may have eternal life.' (RSV)

The Revd William Gulliford

Chaplain to the Bishop of London

I have always found the encounter between Jesus and Nicodemus and the one with the woman of Samaria which follows it, one of the most intensely personal of Jesus' encounters with individuals. The figure of Nicodemus fascinates me. He is a leitmotif in the Gospel of John, appearing at crucial moments in the narrative. As an intellectual, he is drawn to Jesus' persuasive arguments but can never bring himself to proclaim himself a follower of Jesus. In many ways he is a shadowy character, coming to Jesus by night and later being responsible for Jesus' burial, as day is drawing to its close.

The call to Nicodemus is to be reborn. A call he wilfully takes at face value and at which he scoffs. This call clearly haunts Nicodemus for the rest of Jesus' ministry. This call – accompanied by the vivid prefiguring of Jesus of his own death when he says in verse 13 that 'The Son of Man must be lifted up as Moses lifted up the serpent in the wilderness' – encapsulates the work Jesus has come to accomplish. I suppose Nicodemus represents for me those shadowy, yet-to-be-converted parts of myself which long to believe and fail to make adequate testimony of that conviction.

The Rt. Revd Richard Lewis

The Bishop of St Edmundsbury and Ipswich

The reason for choosing the story is because it gives a rare insight into a very personal conversation between Jesus and a respected church leader. The church leader wants a very precise set of answers to his questions but Jesus just keeps giving him answers to a different set of questions!

Verse 8 is a lovely reminder that the Spirit of God will not be controlled and restricted by human beings who want to tie everything down. It blows where it wills and so it is with all who are born of the Spirit.

John 3:16

For God so loved the world, that he gave his only begotten Son, that whosoever believeth in him should not perish, but have everlasting life. (AV)

The Revd Dr Leslie Griffiths
Superintendent Minister of Wesley's Chapel and Former President of the Methodist Conference, 1994–95
I have chosen this verse because in my congregation, we once invited anyone who could recite these words in a language other than English to do so. We heard the familiar cadences in twenty different tongues. Truly God loved the world, the *whole* world.

Kathy Staff
Actress
I think this is wonderful – that God promises everlasting life to all who believe.

John 3:16

For God so loved the world that he gave his only Son, so that everyone who believes in him may not perish but may have eternal life. (NRSV)

and

2 Corinthians 5:17

So if anyone is in Christ, there is a new creation: everything old has passed away; see, everything has become new! (NRSV)

The Revd John Johansen-Berg
Leader of the Community for Reconciliation and Minister of the Beacon Church Centre (United Reformed), Rubery

These two passages show that the divine plan of salvation is personal, social and cosmic. God, Creator and Parent, loves the world and all of its people. He sends his Son for our salvation and for the sake of his whole creation. He longs for us to make right choices, to choose light not darkness, life not death.

When we respond to his love in Christ, there is a new creation. We are renewed; also the universe is renewed.

This is a key message for our generation when the planet is in danger of destruction. We are challenged to work for justice, for peace and for the proper care of our lovely planet Earth.

John 6:12

Gather up the fragments left over, so that nothing may be lost. (NRSV)

THE RT. REVD IAN BRACKLEY

THE BISHOP OF DORKING

I love preaching on this text. It relates to the feeding of the 5,000 but may also be understood to relate to the fragmented experiences of our lives – indeed of all creation. Nothing is lost in the economy of God. All is gathered up ultimately and redeemed and made whole.

~

John 8:11

She said, No man, Lord. And Jesus said unto her, Neither do I condemn thee: go, and sin no more. (AV)

Captain Charles King
Editor of Salvationist *and Contributor on* Pause for Thought, *BBC Radio 2*
This epitomises the 'gospel of the second chance' that the Christian faith is all about. In a very judgmental world these words of Jesus remind us that the future is more important than the past. A favourite couplet of mine is: 'A star is there that once is seen, we may always be what we might have been.' This verse reminds me that, by God's grace, redemption – a fresh start – is always possible.

John 8:32

You will know the truth, and the truth will set you free. (REB)

Dr Peter Vardy
Vice-Principal, Heythrop College, University of London

As soon as truth becomes a dirty word, as soon as truth is ignored, is regarded as irrelevant or even claimed not to exist, then the dehumanising process begins. Facing the truth about ourselves (our childhood, failures, our broken relationships, the hurts we have inflicted as well as the many positive things); about our world (our selfishness, disregard for those in need and for the environment, failure to really care for our neighbours as well as our occasional acts of kindness and love); and about our religious beliefs (about the inadequacies of our church structure, about God and our failure to place God at the centre of our lives as well as the problems of evil and innocent suffering) will always be painful. Most of us prefer to live a lie, to live in the 'comfort zone' of self-deceit. The Gospel verse calls us to a freedom that can only be found in actually seeking truth above everything else and refusing to compromise – no matter what the cost. The price of attempting this is great, but it is only in so doing that real freedom can be found.

~

John 10:10

The thief cometh not, but for to steal, and to kill, and to destroy: I am come that they might have life, and that they might have it more abundantly. (AV)

and

Isaiah 40:31

But they that wait upon the Lord shall renew their strength; they shall mount up with wings as eagles; they shall run, and not be weary; and they shall walk, and not faint. (AV)

The Rt. Revd Alan Chesters
The Bishop of Blackburn
I have chosen St John because for me it sums up the whole purpose of our faith – what Christ brings to our lives; and I have chosen Isaiah because it is such a strength in times when the road is hard and I feel weary.

~

John 10:10

I have come in order that you might have life – life in all its fullness. (GNB)

and

Mark 12:30–31

Love the Lord your God with all your heart, with all your soul, with all your mind, and with all your strength . . . Love your neighbour as you love yourself. (GNB)

THE REVD NIGEL UDEN

MODERATOR OF THE SOUTHERN SYNOD, THE UNITED REFORMED CHURCH

The passage from St John speaks of God the giver of life, wanting us to have the best sort of life we can.

The passage from St Mark speaks of a life in which we know that we are loved by God and by those around us and a life in which we are willing/able to offer love to God and to one another.

THE RT. REVD JOHN OLIVER

THE BISHOP OF HEREFORD

John 10:10 is a verse which I use every time I take a confirmation service, because I believe that it is such a positive and encouraging text on which to end my address to the candidates.

I ask the candidates to remember it if they possibly can, and to remind me of it whenever I see them. It is quite remarkable how many people have said to me, 'John 10:10' on numerous occasions. Sometimes in church, but sometimes in other contexts, in the street, in a shop, on a train, in a car park and so on. It seems to me to encapsulate the good news that Jesus came to be and to do, in a way which is very readily memorable and helpful to those who are embarking on a new stage of their Christian life as confirmed Christians.

John 14:1–7

Let not your heart be troubled: ye believe in God, believe also in me.

In my Father's house are many mansions: if it were not so, I would have told you. I go to prepare a place for you.

And if I go and prepare a place for you, I will come again, and receive you unto myself; that where I am, there ye may be also.

And whither I go ye know, and the way ye know.

Thomas saith unto him, Lord, we know not whither thou goest; and how can we know the way?

Jesus saith unto him, I am the way, the truth, and the life: no man cometh unto the Father, but by me.

If ye had known me, ye should have known my Father also: and from henceforth ye know him, and have seen him. (AV)

Cannon and Ball

Entertainers

Within this seemingly simple verse (6) Jesus tells us all what Christianity is all about. He says that he is *the way* (it is only through Jesus that we will find salvation); *the truth* (when we come to Jesus and offer our sins to him, he takes our sins and makes us new; it is only then when Jesus touches our spirits that we realise the truth – that Jesus is alive and what he tells us through the Bible is true); *the life* (we don't believe that God gives us life for seventy-five years or so then takes it away; everything with God is eternal so that means that once we have had our sins washed in the blood of Christ then we shall live for eternity with Jesus). *No one* (that means exactly what it says): No one can enter into the kingdom of heaven unless they have first had their sins forgiven through Jesus Christ.

John Cole
Writer and Broadcaster

The first few verses of John 14 are Christ's assurance of our eternal life. We cannot know what form this takes, but the assurance is firm. The middle section is a discussion with disciples of their role after his death. From John 14:16 onward, we have the wonderful, again comforting assurances about the Holy Spirit and Christ's promise to leave his peace with us. John 14 contains the central Christian values.

His Eminence Cardinal Cormac Murphy-O'Connor
The Archbishop of Westminster

I find these verses an encouragement in difficult times.

❧

John 15:5

I am the vine, you are the branches. Those who abide in me and I in them bear much fruit, because apart from me you can do nothing. (NRSV)

The Revd Bill Snelson

General Secretary of Churches Together in England

My work as General Secretary of Churches Together in England means spending much of my time with the organisation of the churches, their officers and committees. I need to be reminded that we are brought together in Christ, as interdependent parts of one body; one vine, of which we are branches. And any success we have is thanks to his life and inspiration.

John 15:12–17

This is my commandment: love one another, as I have loved you. There is no greater love than this, that someone should lay down his life for his friends. You are my friends, if you do what I command you. No longer do I call you servants, for a servant does not know what his master is about. I have called you friends, because I have disclosed to you everything that I heard from my Father. You did not choose me: I chose you. I appointed you to go on and bear fruit, fruit that will last; so that the Father may give you whatever you ask in my name. This is my commandment to you: love one another. (REB)

Fern Britton
TV Presenter
This piece sums up the life and work of Jesus for me. I believe the *only* message is to love one another. It should be so simple but it can be so hard. I wish I had met Jesus when he was on Earth, and I wish we could know more about him as a man.

The Rt. Revd Roy Williamson
Hon. Assistant Bishop of Southwell
Formerly the Bishop of Bradford, 1984–91 and the Bishop of Southwark, 1991–98
The Bible is a dynamic book in that it seems to speak pertinently to us in a great variety of situations. I, therefore, have very many favourite texts – texts which have helped me in time of joy, sorrow, failure, success, danger, illness, uncertainty and doubt.

Verse 16 is a particular favourite and reminds me of the initiatives of God in shaping and directing my life and work. It also serves to keep me humble and to accept that the privilege of being called or chosen by God is accompanied by a corresponding responsibility to live for him. In life, privilege and responsibility go hand in hand.

John 16:33

These things I have spoken unto you, that in me ye might have peace. In the world ye shall have tribulation: but be of good cheer; I have overcome the world. (AV)

Colin Dexter

Author

It's like seeing a replay of a soccer match on the telly when your own favourite team is 5–0 down at half time; but you *know* the result already: your own team will end up winning splendidly. (The perfect tense: I already *have* overcome).

~

John 17:20

Neither pray I for these alone, but for them also which shall believe on me through their word. (AV)

Fiona Castle

Author

It is so wonderful to know that Jesus was praying for us before he was crucified. He challenged his disciples to 'Go into all the world and make disciples' (Matthew 28:19) and it is because of their obedience that we know Jesus today. Therefore we should rise to the same challenge for the sake of others who need to hear of him in the future.

John 20:1–16

The first day of the week cometh Mary Magdalene early, when it was yet dark, unto the sepulchre, and seeth the stone taken away from the sepulchre.

Then she runneth, and cometh to Simon Peter, and to the other disciple, whom Jesus loved, and saith unto them, They have taken away the Lord out of the sepulchre, and we know not where they have laid him.

Peter therefore went forth, and that other disciple, and came to the sepulchre.

So they ran both together: and the other disciple did outrun Peter and came first to the sepulchre.

And he stooping down, and looking in, saw the linen clothes lying; yet went he not in.

Then cometh Simon Peter following him, and went into the sepulchre, and seeth the linen clothes lie,

And the napkin, that was about his head, not lying with the linen clothes but wrapped together in a place by itself.

Then went in also that other disciple, which came first to the sepulchre, and he saw, and believed.

For as yet they knew not the scripture, that he must rise again from the dead.

Then the disciples went away again unto their own home.

But Mary stood without at the sepulchre weeping: and as she wept, she stooped down, and looked into the sepulchre,

And seeth two angels in white sitting, the one at the head, and the other at the feet, where the body of Jesus had lain.

And they say unto her, Woman, why weepest thou? She saith unto them, Because they have taken away my Lord, and I know not where they have laid him.

And when she had thus said, she turned herself back, and saw Jesus standing, and knew not that it was Jesus.

Jesus saith unto her, Woman, why weepest thou? whom seekest thou? She, supposing him to be the gardener, saith unto him, Sir, if thou have borne him hence, tell me where thou hast laid him, and I will take him away.

Jesus saith unto her, Mary. She turned herself, and saith unto him, Rabboni; which is to say, Master. (AV)

Sarah Harrison
Author

It's a mixture of mystery and narrative detail.
The sense of early morning hush.
'Supposing him to be the gardener . . .'
The impulsive, emotional, directness of Mary.
The sense that *this* moment was really when it all started.

The Rt. Revd Christopher Herbert
The Bishop of St Albans

I love the way, in verse 15, in which God's humility and self-effacing compassion are revealed. Even after the glory of the resurrection, the Risen Christ is mistaken for a jobbing gardener. It is both beautiful conceptually and also as a story.

John 21:18

Verily, verily, I say unto thee, When thou wast young, thou girdest thyself, and walkedst whither thou wouldest: but when thou shalt be old, thou shalt stretch forth thy hands, and another shall gird thee, and carry thee whither thou wouldest not. (AV)

Margaret Drabble

Novelist

This verse has a mysterious note of tragic resignation and hope. It describes the human condition, the fate of us all. It is about old age, destiny, acceptance and an unknown destination. I find it very moving.

~

Romans 8:28

And we know that all things work together for good to them that love God, to them who are the called according to his purpose. (AV)

Susan Howatch

Novelist

It was the motif of *Absolute Truths*, my final novel in the Starbridge series (six novels about the Church of England in the mid-twentieth century).

The Rt. Revd Keith Sutton

The Bishop of Lichfield

It reminds us that God's loving will and purpose works for us through the difficult times as well as through the good times.

Vice Admiral Sir Peter Woodhead, KCB

Prisons Ombudsman, 1994–99

I have been through good times and not so good times. At present I am in great pain, suffering the after-effects of an operation which has not gone as planned. But I know through my previous experiences that, although at the time one can doubt it, looking back God uses *all* our times to mature us; to help us to be more like Jesus.

Romans 8:37–39

Nay, in all these things we are more than conquerors through him that loved us.

For I am persuaded, that neither death, nor life, nor angels, nor principalities, nor powers, nor things present, nor things to come,

Nor height, nor depth, nor any other creature, shall be able to separate us from the love of God, which is in Christ Jesus our Lord. (AV)

The Ven. John Blackburn, QHC, FRSA
Chaplain-General, HM Land Forces
Army chaplains and soldiers see the good, the bad and the ugly in various countries across the world. Whether in war or peace, hatred or love, pain or pleasure, death or life, these verses speak of the hope we find through God in Christ.

Romans 11:33

O the depth of the riches both of the wisdom and knowledge of God! How unsearchable are his judgments, and his ways past finding out! (AV)

The Rt. Revd Hugh Montefiore
Retired Bishop
It sums up for me the transcendent majesty of God.

Romans 12:9–21

Let love be without dissimulation. Abhor that which is evil; cleave to that which is good.

Be kindly affectioned one to another with brotherly love; in honour preferring one another;

Not slothful in business; fervent in spirit; serving the Lord;

Rejoicing in hope; patient in tribulation; continuing instant in prayer;

Distributing to the necessity of saints; given to hospitality.

Bless them which persecute you: bless, and curse not.

Rejoice with them that do rejoice, and weep with them that weep.

Be of the same mind one toward another. Mind not high things, but condescend to men of low estate. Be not wise in your own conceits.

Recompense to no man evil for evil. Provide things honest in the sight of all men.

If it be possible, as much as lieth in you, live peaceably with all men.

Dearly beloved, avenge not yourselves, but rather give place unto wrath: for it is written, Vengeance is mine; I will repay, saith the Lord.

Therefore if thine enemy hunger, feed him; if he thirst, give him drink: for in so doing thou shalt heap coals of fire on his head.

Be not overcome of evil, but overcome evil with good. (AV)

William Roache, MBE

Actor

It gives good values by which to live. We should all want to help others more and dedicate ourselves to some service. Sadly spiritual matters are rarely talked about. If we all brought out our spiritual selves then all the world's problems would be sorted at a stroke.

~

Romans 12:16

Live in peace with each other. Do not be proud, but make friends with those who seem unimportant. Do not think how clever you are. (YB)

Lisa Potts, GM

Former Nursery Nurse

I think that if we all tried to live out what this verse says, the world and the people who live in it would be so much happier. I think that we spend so much time with our own circle of friends we forget to step out and approach others who aren't the same as us. I have found that sometimes when we make the effort with others who we don't know, but judge them by their cover, they turn out to be so interesting and funny and I sometimes wished I had made the effort earlier. Now I always make friends with people who are different than my own circle of friends.

1 Corinthians 1:9

God is to be trusted, the God who called you to have fellowship with his Son Jesus Christ, our Lord. (GNB)

The Rt. Revd Christopher Mayfield
The Bishop of Manchester
Ever since I discovered the friendship of Jesus for all people – including me – I have sought to serve him as Lord of all, Lord of creation, Lord of history, Lord of eternity. Although I often fail to serve him, God who called me into his friendship continues to forgive and to strengthen me. He is to be trusted!

1 Corinthians 12:4–13

There are different kinds of spiritual gifts, but the same Spirit gives them. There are different ways of serving, but the same Lord is served. There are different abilities to perform service, but the same God gives ability to all for their particular service. The Spirit's presence is shown in some way in each person for the good of all. The Spirit gives one person a message full of wisdom, while to another person the same Spirit gives a message full of knowledge. One and the same Spirit gives faith to one person, while to another person he gives the power to heal. The Spirit gives one person the power to work miracles; to another, the gift of speaking God's message; and to yet another, the ability to tell the difference between gifts that come from the Spirit and those that do not. To one person he gives the ability to speak in strange tongues, and to another he gives the ability to explain what is said. But it is one and the same Spirit who does all this; as he wishes, he gives a different gift to each person.

Christ is like a single body, which has many parts; it is still one body, even though it is made up of different parts. In the same way, all of us, whether Jews or Gentiles, whether slaves or free, have been baptized into the one body by the same Spirit, and we have all been given the one Spirit to drink. (GNB)

THE RT. REVD MARK SANTER

THE BISHOP OF BIRMINGHAM

The passage is a particular favourite of mine because it talks of our interdependence in the Church and how our many gifts can combine to serve Jesus Christ to our best ability.

J. P. R. Williams

Consultant Orthopaedic Surgeon and Former Welsh Rugby International Player, 1969–81

I read this in church recently and it reminded me very much of the relationship between Christ and the human body.

1 Corinthians 12:31– 13:13

But covet earnestly the best gifts: and yet shew I unto you a more excellent way.

Though I speak with the tongues of men and of angels, and have not charity, I am become as sounding brass, or a tinkling cymbal.

And though I have the gift of prophecy, and understand all mysteries, and all knowledge; and though I have all faith, so that I could remove mountains, and have not charity, I am nothing.

And though I bestow all my goods to feed the poor, and though I give my body to be burned, and have not charity, it profiteth me nothing.

Charity suffereth long, and is kind; charity envieth not; charity vaunteth not itself, is not puffed up,

Doth not behave itself unseemly, seeketh not her own, is not easily provoked, thinketh no evil;

Rejoiceth not in iniquity, but rejoiceth in the truth;

Beareth all things, believeth all things, hopeth all things, endureth all things.

Charity never faileth: but whether there be prophecies, they shall fail; whether there be tongues, they shall cease; whether there be knowledge, it shall vanish away.

For we know in part, and we prophesy in part.

But when that which is perfect is come, then that which is in part shall be done away.

When I was a child, I spake as a child, I understood as a child, I thought as a child: but when I became a man, I put away childish things.

For now we see through a glass, darkly; but then face to face: now I know in part; but then shall I know even as also I am known.

And now abideth faith, hope, charity, these three; but the greatest of these is charity. (AV)

JENNY AGUTTER

ACTRESS

I like the translation that uses charity as opposed to love. It is good to understand what love/charity means.

ROSEMARY CONLEY

DIET AND FITNESS AUTHOR AND BROADCASTER

I believe it encapsulates the whole message of Christianity – love the Lord your God and love your neighbour as yourself. If we have love, we have everything.

TOM COURTENAY

ACTOR

I loved reading it at school aloud, from the stage in assembly.

ADMIRAL SIR NIGEL ESSENHIGH, KCB, ADC

FIRST SEA LORD AND CHIEF OF NAVAL STAFF

I have always viewed the writings of St Paul to be the ones which seem to me to have the greatest relevance to the difficult world in which we now live, 2,000 years after they were penned. They seem to have an enduring quality of pragmatism and common sense which I find helpful.

In particular there are some verses in chapter 13 of 1 Corinthians which sum up what our attitude should be to living in a largely atheistic or at best agnostic and wholly materialistic society.

Clare Francis

Writer

I have chosen this passage for its last line: '. . . but the greatest of these is charity'. Charity encompasses generosity, compassion, forgiveness – the most important qualities of all.

Sir Edward George

The Governor of the Bank of England

I find it very difficult to decide on my favourite anything! Whether it is my favourite picture or poem, hymn or music, food or place, or people, and so on. I find that I have very catholic taste, and my 'favourite' at any particular time depends upon my mood, the surrounding circumstances – including what is on my mind, the company I am with and lots of other factors. But I always rather enjoy asking myself what is my 'favourite' because it makes me remind myself of all the things in the particular category that I like as I try to decide between them. As a result, it can be a very pleasurable, positive experience.

At odd moments over the last few months, I have found myself recalling a whole variety of passages from the Bible, running from the stories and psalms of the Old Testament, through the Gospels to the Acts and Letters of the apostles, and often looking up the references to remind myself of the details of the story or of the precise language. You can imagine how difficult it was to decide on my 'favourite'. But I have finally decided on chapter 13 of Paul's First Epistle to the Corinthians. Even having decided that, I was not and still am not sure whether I prefer it in the authorised 'faith, hope and charity' translation, or in the modern translation of 'faith, hope and love'. I finally came down in favour of the authorised translation.

The reason I reached this conclusion is, of course, importantly to do with the nobility of the thought and the majesty of the language. But it is also because I have a vivid recollection of the first occasion on which it made a huge impression on me as a schoolboy, aged thirteen or fourteen, at Dulwich College, when it was magnificently read, by I think the school captain, at a school service.

Cathy Kelly

Writer

This passage touched me in a way that other verses don't. It seems to me to be what love and true faith are really about.

Cliff Morgan, OBE

International Rugby Union Player for Wales, British Lions and Barbarians, and Head of Outside Broadcasts Group, BBC Television, 1975–87

The last verse of chapter 13 will always be with me.

I chose this because when I was a youngster my mother told me of a wonderful sermon preached by Dr Elfed Lewis, one of the greatest pillars of Welsh nonconformity and a distinguished hymn writer. This was his text. My mother would sing to me one of his hymns:

Arglwydd lesu dysc i'm gerdded
Trwy y byd yn ol dy droed.

'Lord Jesus, teach me to walk the world in your footsteps.'

One night his father was taking him to a prayer meeting. It was very dark and the footpath very narrow. His father, carrying a lantern went before him. Wondering whether the boy was following him safely, he called out: 'Follow in my footsteps and you will be all right.' Years later, Elfed remembered this and wrote the hymn, which asks Jesus to teach us to walk through life by following in his footsteps.

Nicholas Parsons

Actor and Broadcaster

This chapter expresses most movingly in beautifully phrased language what love – or charity as it was called then – is all about, and how it is the most essential quality for any human being to possess.

Angela Thorne

Actress

This whole chapter is *so* beautifully dramatic, *so* full of wisdom and *so* profound. It makes me tingle when I read it and brings a huge lump to my throat.

Joanna Trollope

Novelist

Everything cited in this chapter seems not only to be both eternal and universal in its application, but also for most of us to be at least in some degree possible.

2 Corinthians 4:1–10

Since God in his mercy has given us this ministry, we never lose heart. We have renounced the deeds that people hide for very shame; we do not practise cunning or distort the word of God. It is by declaring the truth openly that we recommend ourselves to the conscience of our fellow-men in the sight of God. If our gospel is veiled at all, it is veiled only for those on the way to destruction; their unbelieving minds are so blinded by the god of this passing age that the gospel of the glory of Christ, who is the image of God, cannot dawn upon them and bring them light. It is not ourselves that we proclaim; we proclaim Christ Jesus as Lord, and ourselves as your servants for Jesus's sake. For the God who said, 'Out of darkness light shall shine,' has caused his light to shine in our hearts, the light which is knowledge of the glory of God in the face of Jesus Christ.

But we have only earthenware jars to hold this treasure, and this proves that such transcendent power does not come from us; it is God's alone. We are hard pressed, but never cornered; bewildered, but never at our wits' end; hunted, but never abandoned to our fate; struck down, but never killed. Wherever we go we carry with us in our body the death that Jesus died, so that in this body also the life that Jesus lives may be revealed. (REB)

The Rt. Revd Nigel McCulloch

The Bishop of Wakefield

I have chosen this passage because, at times in my life when things have been difficult and I have felt down, these words have helped and encouraged me. Much to my surprise, I discovered that this passage, so well known to me, is read at the lesson during the service of the consecration of a bishop. Perhaps the compilers of the service realised that even bishops need to be encouraged!

The Rt. Revd Martin Wharton

The Bishop of Newcastle

These verses were read at my ordination as a bishop and have always been special for me – not least because of the key verse, 'It is not ourselves that we proclaim; we proclaim Christ Jesus as Lord, and ourselves as your servants for Jesus's sake' – which is the duty laid upon all Christian people.

~

2 Corinthians 4:13

We having the same spirit of faith, according as it is written, I believed, and therefore have I spoken; we also believe, and therefore speak. (AV)

The Rt. Hon. Ann Widdecombe MP
The verse is an exhortation to courage, to speaking out, and not to hide one's light under a bushel.

2 Corinthians 5:16–21

With us therefore worldly standards have ceased to count in our estimate of anyone; even if once they counted in our understanding of Christ, they do so now no longer. For anyone united to Christ, there is a new creation: the old order has gone; a new order has already begun.

All this has been the work of God. He has reconciled us to himself through Christ, and has enlisted us in this ministry of reconciliation: God was in Christ reconciling the world to himself, no longer holding people's misdeeds against them, and has entrusted us with the message of reconciliation. We are therefore Christ's ambassadors. It is as if God were appealing to you through us: we implore you in Christ's name, be reconciled to God! Christ was innocent of sin, and yet for our sake God made him one with human sinfulness, so that in him we might be made one with the righteousness of God. (REB)

The Rt. Revd Dr Peter Forster

The Bishop of Chester

This passage speaks of God's love for the whole world, and of our participation in God's work as his ambassadors.

The Revd Elizabeth Welch

Moderator of the United Reformed Church, 2001–02

Verses 18 and 19 speak to me of the hope we have in Jesus Christ, that we as individuals can be reconciled to God and that people who are divided can be reconciled to each other. It also speaks to me of the role each one of us is called to play in working for reconciliation whether between individuals or among nations.

2 Corinthians 6:3–10

Giving no offence in any thing, that the ministry be not blamed:

But in all things approving ourselves as the ministers of God, in much patience, in afflictions, in necessities, in distresses.

In stripes, in imprisonments, in tumults, in labours, in watchings, in fastings;

By pureness, by knowledge, by longsuffering, by kindness, by the Holy Ghost, by love unfeigned.

By the word of truth, by the power of God, by the armour of righteousness on the right hand and on the left.

By honour and dishonour, by evil report and good report: as deceivers, and yet true;

As unknown, and yet well known; as dying, and, behold, we live; as chastened, and not killed;

As sorrowful, yet alway rejoicing; as poor, yet making many rich; as having nothing, and yet possessing all things. (AV)

The Rt. Revd Thomas Butler
The Bishop of Southwark
I have chosen this passage because it reminds us of the cost and the joy of Christian discipleship.

2 Corinthians 12:9

But his answer was: 'My grace is all you need; power is most fully seen in weakness.' I am therefore happy to boast of my weaknesses, because then the power of Christ will rest upon me. (REB)

The Rt. Revd Lord David Sheppard of Liverpool

England Cricketer, 1950–63, and The Bishop of Liverpool, 1975–97

Sometimes Christians seem to expect that, if they trust in God, they should always prosper and have perfect health. In this part of his letter to the Corinthians, St Paul says he was given a 'thorn in the flesh'. Three times he begged God to take it away, but he received the answer in the text I have chosen. No one knows just what the 'thorn in the flesh' was, but physical weakness or sickness – or a struggle in life – is what many loyal Christians face, and the text is a great encouragement. I have personally found it a great resource at moments when life has been a struggle.

~

Galatians 2:20

I am crucified with Christ: nevertheless I live; yet not I, but Christ liveth in me: and the life which I now live in the flesh I live by the faith of the Son of God, who loved me, and gave himself for me. (AV)

Jonathan Edwards
Athlete
Triple Jump Olympic Gold Medallist
It encapsulates how I try to live my life.

The Revd David Winter
Minister, Author and Broadcaster
It is 'religion' made personal – and St Paul is angry with the Galatian Christians but for a moment he forgets his anger at this wonder of the truth that the Son of God actually loved *him*, and gave his life for *him*.

Ephesians 2:19

So then you are no longer strangers and aliens, but you are citizens with the saints and also members of the household of God. (NRSV)

Pauline Webb

(Retired) Broadcaster, Writer and Methodist Lay Preacher

I have chosen this verse because it stresses the fact that we human beings all belong to one family in which no one is a foreigner or treated as an outsider. I belong to a church congregation which is fully multiracial, where we enjoy our fellowship with one another in Christ.

Ephesians 3:14–21

With this in mind, then, I kneel in prayer to the Father, from whom every family in heaven and on earth takes its name, that out of the treasures of his glory he may grant you strength and power through his Spirit in your inner being, that through faith Christ may dwell in your hearts in love. With deep roots and firm foundations, may you be strong to grasp, with all God's people, what is the breadth and length and height and depth of the love of Christ, and to know it, though it is beyond knowledge. So may you attain to fullness of being, the fullness of God himself.

Now to him who is able to do immeasurably more than all we can ask or conceive, by the power which is at work among us, to him be glory in the church and in Christ Jesus from generation to generation evermore! Amen. (NEB)

THE RT. REVD RICHARD HARRIES
THE BISHOP OF OXFORD
This passage sets out such an amazing view of what it is to be a human being. As we grow in understanding of Christ's love for us, we are to be filled with 'the fullness of God himself'.

Ephesians 4:32; 5:1–2

And be ye kind one to another, tenderhearted, forgiving one another; even as God for Christ's sake hath forgiven you.

Be ye therefore followers of God, as dear children;

And walk in love, as Christ also hath loved us, and hath given himself for us an offering and a sacrifice to God for a sweetsmelling savour. (AV)

The Rt. Revd Michael Scott-Joynt
The Bishop of Winchester
For me, this passage catches the heart of God's gift and calling to us of living in the way of Jesus, through him.

Ephesians 6:10–20

Finally, my brethren, be strong in the Lord, and in the power of his might.

Put on the whole armour of God, that ye may be able to stand against the wiles of the devil.

For we wrestle not against flesh and blood, but against principalities, against powers, against the rulers of the darkness of this world, against spiritual wickedness in high places.

Wherefore take unto you the whole armour of God, that ye may be able to withstand in the evil day, and having done all, to stand.

Stand therefore, having your loins girt about with truth, and having on the breastplate of righteousness.

And your feet shod with the preparation of the gospel of peace.

Above all, taking the shield of faith, wherewith ye shall be able to quench all the fiery darts of the wicked.

And take the helmet of salvation, and the sword of the Spirit, which is the word of God;

Praying always with all prayer and supplication in the Spirit, and watching thereunto with all perseverance and supplication for all saints;

And for me, that utterance may be given unto me, that I may open my mouth boldly, to make known the mystery of the gospel.

For which I am an ambassador in bonds: that therein I may speak boldly, as I ought to speak. (AV)

The Ven. John Blackburn, QHC, FRSA

Chaplain-General, HM Land Forces

Army chaplains and the soldiers they minister to are often faced with tough situations. Running away is not an option. These verses speak of God's armour defending us and God's strength encouraging us to stand and face any situation, no matter how difficult.

The Rt. Hon. The Lord David Owen, CH

Former Leader of the Social Democratic Party and the European Union's Peace Envoy in the Balkans

The passage which is most evocative for me comes from St Paul's Epistle to the Ephesians. My grandfather, who was blind from the age of twelve, became a clergyman and was a very remarkable man. He was vicar of Llandow and Lysworney in the Church of Wales. My mother, sister and I moved from Plymouth during the war and lived with my grandparents in Llandow. I remember attending the local school and in order to encourage me to improve my reading and to stand up in public, my grandfather set a date when I would have to read this passage from the Bible in his church. It was his favourite passage from the Bible and it has remained one of mine ever since and one which is identified in my own mind with my first minor achievement.

Philippians 2:1–11

If there be therefore any consolation in Christ, if any comfort of love, if any fellowship of the Spirit, if any bowels and mercies,

Fulfil ye my joy, that ye be likeminded, having the same love, being of one accord, of one mind.

Let nothing be done through strife or vainglory; but in lowliness of mind let each esteem other better than themselves.

Look not every man on his own things, but every man also on the things of others.

Let this mind be in you, which was also in Christ Jesus:

Who, being in the form of God, thought it not robbery to be equal with God:

But made himself of no reputation, and took upon him the form of a servant, and was made in the likeness of men:

And being found in fashion as a man, he humbled himself, and became obedient unto death, even the death of the cross.

Wherefore God also hath highly exalted him, and given him a name which is above every name:

That at the name of Jesus every knee should bow, of things in heaven, and things in earth, and things under the earth;

And that every tongue should confess that Jesus Christ is Lord, to the glory of God the Father. (AV)

The Revd David Helyar

Former Southern Synod Moderator of the United Reformed Church

The passage speaks of the uniqueness of Christ – his humility, suffering and obedience which alone can lead to his being exalted as Lord of all time and space. Our own attitudes and lifestyle must follow Christ's, leading us to humility and love in all our relationships.

Philippians 4:4–8

Rejoice in the Lord alway: and again I say, Rejoice.

Let your moderation be known unto all men. The Lord is at hand.

Be careful for nothing; but in every thing by prayer and supplication with thanksgiving let your requests be made known unto God.

And the peace of God, which passeth all understanding, shall keep your hearts and minds through Christ Jesus.

Finally, brethren, whatsoever things are true, whatsoever things are honest, whatsoever things are just, whatsoever things are pure, whatsoever things are lovely, whatsoever things are of good report; if there be any virtue, and if there be any praise, think on these things. (AV)

THE REVD ANTHONY BURNHAM

FORMER GENERAL SECRETARY OF THE UNITED REFORMED CHURCH AND MODERATOR OF THE FREE CHURCHES' COUNCIL

I had to learn Verses 7 and 8 at school as an eight-year-old. Fifty years later they still speak to me. Verse 7 speaks of the gift of God's peace and verse 8 of our need to respond and how!

WENDY CRAIG

ACTRESS

My profession is one which is often tense and fraught. Praying and praising bring me close to the Father and help to keep fear and anxiety at bay. When we trust him, God gives us courage, calm and joy.

Sue McGregor

BBC Radio Broadcaster, Today *Programme*

Verse 8 is a reminder to us cynical journalists that there is good in our 'wicked' world, even if we don't often find time to report it.

Philippians 4:4–9

I want you to be happy, always happy in the Lord; I repeat, what I want is your happiness. Let your tolerance be evident to everyone: the Lord is very near. There is no need to worry; but if there is anything you need, pray for it, asking God for it with prayer and thanksgiving, and that peace of God, which is so much greater than we can understand, will guard your hearts and your thoughts, in Christ Jesus. Finally, brothers, fill your minds with everything that is true, everything that is noble, everything that is good and pure, everything that we love and honour, and everything that can be thought virtuous or worthy of praise. Keep doing all the things that you learnt from me and have been taught by me and have heard or seen that I do. Then the God of peace will be with you. (JB)

FATHER BRIAN D'ARCY, CP

PRIEST AND BROADCASTER

The reasons I have chosen this passage are manifold. For a start, the advice is down to earth and sensible in the extreme.

But its impact has always been an antidote to the normal perception of what religion encourages. We are advised to be happy. Frequently religion seems to trade in misery.

Yet here is the word of God telling us to be happy and in case we missed it the first time, repeating the message 'all I want is your happiness'. How comforting.

The passage then goes on to tell me why I should be happy. First of all it presumes I have good sense and tolerance which I should share with everybody else. But really the happiness is based on the fact that the Lord is very near. So there is no need to worry. But God understands that I will still worry.

So then he gives me a step-by-step guide to overcome the worry. I should pray for it. I should ask God for it and then thank God. The promise is wonderful. The peace of God which surpasses all our understanding will guard our hearts and our thoughts. No wonder we are allowed to be happy.

And as always when we recognise how many gifts God has given to us we'll be grateful for them. And that's why we should fill our minds with everything that is true and noble and good and pure.

I spend my life searching for peace in the bits and pieces of every day. These verses from Philippians are a source of enormous strength and consolation to me, especially in times of sadness in my life.

Philippians 4:13

I can do all things through him who strengthens me. (NRSV)

THE MOST REVD AND RT. HON. GEORGE CAREY

THE ARCHBISHOP OF CANTERBURY, 1991–2002

Christ does not promise his followers an easy time, but he does promise to be with us always and to give us the strength to serve him faithfully. I have always been deeply encouraged by the memorable way in which St Paul expresses this important aspect of Christian experience.

This passage was also chosen by
SIR CLIFF RICHARD, OBE
SINGER

Colossians 3:15–17

And let the peace of God rule in your hearts, to the which also ye are called in one body; and be ye thankful.

Let the word of Christ dwell in you richly in all wisdom; teaching and admonishing one another in psalms and hymns and spiritual songs, singing with grace in your hearts to the Lord.

And whatsoever ye do in word or deed, do all in the name of the Lord Jesus, giving thanks to God and the Father by him. (AV)

THE RT. REVD COLIN BUCHANAN
THE BISHOP OF WOOLWICH
This passage has many depths of meaning, is centred in Jesus Christ, is outworked in the life of both Church and individuals, and keeps coming back to me.

1 Thessalonians 5:24

He who calls you is faithful, and he will do it. (RSV)

The Revd Christina Le Moignan

Methodist Minister and President of the Methodist Conference, 2001–02

This verse assures me first that God is doing something in this world (which needs him so badly); and second that I have a part to play in this, but that it does not depend on me. (If it did, I would give up because it is beyond me.)

2 Timothy 1:2–7

To Timothy his dear son.

Grace, mercy, and peace to you from God the Father and our Lord Jesus Christ.

I thank God – whom I, like my forefathers, worship with a pure intention – when I mention you in my prayers; this I do constantly night and day. And when I remember the tears you shed, I long to see you again to make my happiness complete. I am reminded of the sincerity of your faith, a faith which was alive in Lois your grandmother and Eunice your mother before you, and which, I am confident, lives in you also.

That is why I now remind you to stir into flame the gift of God which is within you through the laying on of my hands. For the spirit that God gave us is no craven spirit, but one to inspire strength, love, and self-discipline. (NEB)

Sir Henry Cooper, OBE, KSG

Professional Boxer, 1954–71

Being a Christian family I can acknowledge many passages which have inspired me over the years. However, I suggest this passage as a source of enlightenment.

The Rt. Revd Michael Turnbull

The Bishop of Durham

Verse 6 'stir into flame the gift of God which is within you' has always reminded me that all we do is the result of God's initiative with us, but he expects us to use God's resources and keep him fresh and alive. I keep it in a frame in my view from my desk.

~

Hebrews 11:13–16

These all died in faith, not having received the promises, but having seen them afar off, and were persuaded of them, and embraced them, and confessed that they were strangers and pilgrims on the earth.

For they that say such things declare plainly that they seek a country.

And truly, if they had been mindful of that country from whence they came out, they might have had opportunity to have returned.

But now they desire a better country, that is an heavenly: wherefore God is not ashamed to be called their God: for he hath prepared for them a city. (AV)

The Rt. Revd Peter Selby
The Bishop of Worcester
It is such an inspiring statement about God's beckoning us to an unknown future.

Hebrews 13:1–6

Keep on loving each other as brothers. Do not forget to entertain strangers, for by so doing some people have entertained angels without knowing it. Remember those in prison as if you were their fellow-prisoners, and those who are ill-treated as if you yourselves were suffering.

Marriage should be honoured by all, and the marriage bed kept pure, for God will judge the adulterer and all the sexually immoral. Keep your lives free from the love of money and be content with what you have, because God has said,

'Never will I leave you;
never will I forsake you.'

So we say with confidence,

'The Lord is my helper; I will not be afraid.
What can man do to me?' (NIV)

Leslie Grantham
Actor
This passage shows that love can conquer all.

~

James 1:19

Let every man be quick to hear, slow to speak, slow to anger. (RSV)

COLIN BAKER

ACTOR

It is very good simple advice – although sometimes difficult to adhere to.

~

James 2:15–17

Suppose a brother or sister is without clothes and daily food. If one of you says to him, 'Go, I wish you well; keep warm and well fed,' but does nothing about his physical needs, what good is it? In the same way, faith by itself, if it is not accompanied by action, is dead. (NIV)

Peter Barkworth

Actor

It says there is no point in having lovely, pious, generalised thoughts about other people unless you convert those thoughts into generous actions.

1 Peter 2:9–10

But ye are a chosen generation, a royal priesthood, an holy nation, a peculiar people; that ye should shew forth the praises of him who hath called you out of darkness into his marvellous light:

Which in time past were not a people, but are now the people of God: which had not obtained mercy, but have now obtained mercy. (AV)

THE RT. REVD DAVID BENTLEY

THE BISHOP OF GLOUCESTER

It is a very fine description of the Church as composed of ordinary people 'chosen' by God for various forms of ministry. It is a passage that is often used at the many confirmation services I conduct each year.

~

1 John 3:16

Hereby perceive we the love of God, because he laid down his life for us: and we ought to lay down our lives for the brethren. (AV)

Jonathan Edwards
Athlete
Triple Jump Olympic Gold Medallist
It speaks of God's love for us in sending Jesus to die on a cross for our sins and also gives us that sacrifice as a standard for the way we love others.

~

1 John 4:16–21

And we have known and believed the love that God hath to us. God is love; and he that dwelleth in love dwelleth in God, and God in him.

Herein is our love made perfect, that we may have boldness in the day of judgment: because as he is, so are we in this world.

There is no fear in love; but perfect love casteth out fear: because fear hath torment. He that feareth is not made perfect in love.

We love him, because he first loved us.

If a man say, I love God, and hateth his brother, he is a liar: for he that loveth not his brother whom he hath seen, how can he love God whom he hath not seen?

And this commandment have we from him, That he who loveth God love his brother also. (AV)

Princess Michael of Kent
Her Royal Highness feels that it is the love of God for us all that is at the core of her religion.

Revelation 21:1–4

And I saw a new heaven and a new earth: for the first heaven and the first earth were passed away; and there was no more sea.

And I John saw the holy city, new Jerusalem, coming down from God out of heaven, prepared as a bride adorned for her husband.

And I heard a great voice out of heaven saying, Behold, the tabernacle of God is with men, and he will dwell with them, and they shall be his people, and God himself shall be with them, and be their God.

And God shall wipe away all tears from their eyes; and there shall be no more death, neither sorrow, nor crying, neither shall there be any more pain: for the former things are passed away. (AV)

Chris Curtis

Headteacher, St Bede's School, Redhill, Surrey

Whenever I read these words, a tune starts in my head. It is the version of this passage that they sing at Turvey Abbey, on some Sunday evenings. I can easily think of such evenings in the spring, when it has been a warm day with a hint of the summer to come. The simple harmonies and the pure voices of the monks and nuns join with the twilight outside the chapel window and the words fill you with such deep longing. You long for summer after the winter and you long for things to change, for the day to come when all people will finally be as they were meant to be.

I have always had this longing, even as a child. The world is full of so much that is amazing and wonderful, but there is so much trouble and pain and hurt mixed in. You see this so clearly in any big city – humanity at its most impressive and at its worst – but beyond all this confusion, this strange mixture of good and bad, there is a loving God who will bring in what we all long for. We want things to be different. We feel that they are not as they should be and we live in hope that things will change. Putting it another way, we often feel homeless and we are searching for our home.

This passage is full of that hope and an answer to that longing. A simple promise that there is a city that is simply good to live in, where people will be at home. The city will be a gift from God, the place where he will live with us, but this is no abstract or 'spiritual' heaven. There is nothing more human than a city. As always, God comes to us and lives with us. The pain and sadness find their meaning and the good things find their fulfilment.

This passage sums up the whole Christian message, and I long to see it fulfilled, though as a keen sailor, I hope there might be room for at least a little sea after all!

Index of Names

Other gift books published by Hodder:

In Green Pastures

Psalms for Everyday Life

In Green Pastures places you alongside the psalmists of the Bible, and will be a help whether you are giving thanks and praise or wrestling with doubts and questions. Share in the writers' joy and suffering, and in their words discover wisdom, comfort and peace.

Elegantly displayed as poetry and containing the complete Book of Psalms from the New International Version, the world's most popular modern English Bible translation, this volume will be used again and again. Though these words were written more than 2000 years ago, they still inspire the heart, stimulate the mind and comfort the spirit.

Hodder & Stoughton
ISBN 0 340 78662 0

Pause for Thought

Foreword by Terry Wogan
Compiled by Lavinia Byrne

A little book from BBC Radio 2's popular *Pause for Thought*, introduced by Terry Wogan, featuring words of wisdom to comfort and inspire.

'There's nothing automatic about our spiritual life. Growth there is the result of effort: reading and thinking and praying.'
Captain Charles King

'Wherever hungrey people are fed, homeless people sheltered, rejected people welcomed, powerless people empowered, Christ is born again and all heaven breaks loose.'
Revd Ruth Scott

'It was Guru Nanak, the founder of Sikhism, who reminded us that God is not the lease impressed by national or religious identity. It's how we respect and behave to our neighbour that really counts.'
Indarjit Singh

Hodder & Stoughton
ISBN 0 340 86107 X

Something Understood

An Anthology of Poetry and Prose

Introduced by Mark Tully
Compiled by Beverley McAinsh

This richly varied anthology of poems and prose reflects the depth and universality of human experience and is drawn from BBC Radio 4's popular series *Something Understood.*

Introduced by presenter Mark Tully and compiled by producer Beverley McAinsh, the collections spans a rich variety of subjects including: birth; family, friends and lovers; the natural world; visions, dreams and silence; despair and hope; old age and death; heroes, gurus and guides; journeying and pilgrimage – and much more.

This is a book to treasure and to return to again and again, full of universal wisdom.

Hodder & Stoughton
ISBN 0 340 75703 5

Who Do You Say I Am?

The Many Names of Jesus

Eva Chambers and Jennifer Rees Larcombe

" 'What about you?' he asked, 'Who do you say I am?' Simon Peter answered, 'You are the Christ, the Son of the Living God.' "
(Matthew 16:15–16)

Jesus was given many other names in Scripture, including Good Shepherd, Immanuel, Light of the World, Redeemer, Son of Man and Son of God. These names and the characteristics they describe have been reflected in the experiences of millions of people, showing the unique and personal meaning of Jesus for all who have known him.

In this inspirational book Eva Chambers and best-selling author Jennifer Rees Larcombe have collected poems, prayers and individual stories written by men, women and children from across the ages – together they paint a glorious picture of Jesus and illustrate the incredible depth of his character.

Hodder & Stoughton
ISBN 0 340 78581 0

Page 47
Proverbs 4 Wisdom is the principal
thing
1 Corinthians 12-31 - Page 170
Proverbs 31 Page 50 Virtuous woman
Psalm 104 Creation Hymn P33
Proverbs 4 Wisdom is the principal
Page 47 Thing
Psalm 23 P. 23